FRAUD
ON THE
COURT

*One Adoptee's Fight to
Reclaim his Identity*

Mike Chalek

and Jessica Gardner

For inquiries, please visit our website at www.adoption-fraud.com for the most up-to-date contact methods.

Ordering Information:

- Orders by U.S. trade bookstores and wholesalers. Please contact Ingram Book Company.
- Orders by individuals. Purchase online or from your favorite bookstore.

Cover art design by Sanders Design Group

Published by Universal Technical Systems, Inc.

Printed in the United States of America

First Edition, Paperback

ISBN: 978-0-9885351-1-4

Library of Congress Control Number: 2012955206

We wish to dedicate this book to the following individuals, who made this story possible:

To Josette P. Marquess, MSW Coordinator, Florida Adoption Reunion Registry Florida Department of Children and Families - An unusual individual who went to great lengths to do the right thing.

To Mallory E. Horne, a very prominent Florida politician who stood beside me throughout this emotional and legal journey and wasn't afraid to receive an adverse ruling from the courts. I enjoyed the ride and I will miss you.

To Virginia Snyder, private investigator extraordinaire, who tells things as they really are and who has inspired me to pursue my quest for truth.

To Judge Robert P. Cates of Alachua County who made that quantum leap forward to unseal my closed adoption record.

To my missing baby sister, Carol Jean, whom I have never met. One day I hope to solve that mystery as well.

And finally to my mother, Winnie Faye, whom I will never forget despite the brief time that I spent with her.

~Mike

For my family, who gave every spare moment toward making sure I was free to complete this work. And for Larry and Denise, the birth parents of my own adopted children. I hope that from your vantage points in heaven you can see what incredible young men they have all become.

~Jessica

Preface

"What a tangled web we weave when first we practice to deceive."

I have been a prime example of this truism for just about all of my life, something I began to realize at the age of 11. My story involves one of the most well-documented adoption fraud cases that existed in Florida in the early 1950's. There are so many more stories, though, than just mine.

In today's terms the practice of baby selling is known as "human trafficking". In those days known as the Baby Scoop Era, young single women who found themselves pregnant were routinely coerced into giving up their children and frequently encouraged to use fictitious names in doing so. Even when the adoptions were completed legally, the practice of sealing up the records and the original birth certificate was standard. No one, not the doctors, baby brokers, adoptive parents or even state legislators, considered that the baby being sold would not remain an infant, that the child would become an adult with a primal desire to know his or her biological origins.

In my own long quest for the truth, it was in 1995

that a series of unusual events began which involved several prominent individuals in the Florida adoption and legal/judicial circles. These events enabled my twisted story to fully rear its ugly head and to eventually be cut off at the neck. My adoption was reversed, and a sort of justice was granted.

Some of the Florida courts were compromised upon a close examination of their past decisions and their dignity was clearly at stake, but we all should be held accountable for what we do, regardless of our elected positions. I am grateful for that accountability, and it is true in my case that "the truth shall set you free." In my quest to find my identity I was able to achieve that extraordinary freedom that comes with mental closure. I felt that this book should have been written then, at the time of the final ruling, but I just wasn't ready for it and the timing in the universe wasn't there. Instead, in 1999 I created a web site at www.adoption-fraud.com depicting the facts of my case with the hope that I would be helping others who were dealing with similar circumstances.

Over the last ten years I have received *thousands* of emails from adoptees and birth mothers informing me of their difficult plights in wanting to find one another. I was only able to really help a small few of them. But I learned that I was not alone in my experience of a primal need to know who I am biologically and where I fit into the human genealogical tree. It is my belief, as well as that of many others in the adoption triad, that it is not a natural thing for a child to be separated from the first mother. That bond, hidden though it may be, was never meant to be severed for a lifetime. This does *not* mean that real and enduring bonds of family cannot be made with adoptive parents. It simply means that we cannot erase the first family as if it never existed. We may seal up the paper records in a file deep in the bowels of the court, but all the secrecy in the world cannot sever the bonds at the human level.

I used to think that being consumed by the questions of my identity and origins made me an inferior person, even as a child. Questions kept popping into my head. "Do I have other siblings who look like me?" "Is my birth mother still thinking of me?" and "Why did she give me up?" I could only hold those questions inside of me for many years, with no hope of ever finding out. My adoptive parents would never entertain my need for information and the adoptive mother in particular was unusually cruel when faced with the reality of an adopted child's normal curiousity about his "other" family.

This cruelty alone might have provided the emotional steam necessary to drive my investigation for the truth. But there were other forces behind the investigation (besides my own tenacity) that I cannot explain. In other words, the story of my life is so incredible that the casual observer may be overwhelmed by the unlikely sequence of events and the remarkable coincidences that kept things rolling. And yes, truth is stranger than fiction and it always will be.

It took the involvement of powerful individuals within the State of Florida to fully expose the fraudulence of my case and to make the groundbreaking legal decisions possible. I am grateful to have met Mallory Horne, a well-known and highly connected lawyer who was once the Florida Speaker of the House and President of the Florida Senate. If he didn't have a story to tell of his own involving a fraudulent federal investigation that nearly destroyed his career, he probably wouldn't have taken my case. He did take it though, after much persuasion, and we became close friends for the next 10 years until his death in April 2009.

Also of critical importance in my investigation was a wonderful woman named Josette Marquess. Ms. Marquess headed up the adoption reunion registry in Tallahassee and was responsible for revealing non identifying facts to anyone requesting information related to their closed adoption records. She provided me with a five page letter in 1995 detailing some of the extraordinary events surrounding my adoption. In December 1998, I eventually received my 108 page closed adoption record after I filed a pro-se petition to unseal, based on a claim of "Fraud on the Court", using that original five page letter as my sole supporting evidence.

And it was Virginia Snyder, a private investigator in Delray Beach Florida, who inspired me to file that motion to unseal and told me that I was holding the smoking gun. If you ever saw the TV series *Murder, She Wrote*, then you may have a good picture of Virginia. The chronicles in that show mirrored many of her real-life cases. "Gumshoe Granny" (as she is affectionately known) has made many television appearances throughout the years, including on the David Letterman Show. She is still alive today and is 92 years young.

Aside from my own case, I have noticed that the adoption reform movement has gained momentum over the years in a quest to recognize the rights of adoptees nationwide. After all, adoption affects 1 out of every 4 Americans. That is a percentage of the population too large to ignore. For many adoptees, the sealing of our original birth certificates and our adoption files could be called our own "Roswell Cover Up," perpetuated at the hands of the officials that are, or were, in power.

Our stance is that every person has a right to know their origins, and that knowing or not knowing can have an everlasting impact on a person's life. The laws surrounding closed adoptions are a dysfunctional part of America's infrastructure that tear away at the very fabric of a free and democratic society. The courts and legislators need to be better educated, by real members of the adoption triad and not powerful and corrupt special interest lobbyists, so that the modern notion of permanently closed adoptions—and the frequent human trafficking that results—will one day be a tragedy of the past.

Terminology

There is much discussion within the adoption community as to the most appropriate terminology to use when referring to the parents who have given life to a child, but are not the parents who are raising that child.

The same debate also surrounds the terminology used to describe the transfer of a child's care from one set of legal parents to another.

Throughout this book we use the term "birth mother" to refer to the mother of origin, and the term "relinquishment" to describe the act of giving a child to someone else to raise in an adoptive environment.

These terms do not necessarily reflect the views of the authors on the matter. They are simply the most widely recognizable terms in use at this time, and we wish to reach as broad an audience as possible with the message of our book.

We encourage all interested readers to look up more on the nature of this debate by performing a simple internet search or by visiting some of the many forums dedicated to adoption issues.

Language is a powerful tool for framing our perception of ourselves and our world. While the issue of adoption language is far from settled, we support ongoing honest and open discussion that will lead to a better understanding for all involved.

Prologue

This is what I have pieced together of the black market baby ring that, once upon a time, transferred me from my birth mother's care and into the home of Alex and Adela Chalek, with less fuss and procedure than what it now takes to adopt a pet from the local animal shelter.

In the 1950s, in Jacksonville FL, lived one Charles and Lenora Fielding of 143 Talullah Avenue. Charles was a local police captain, had been on the force for some 30 years, and was as well known (and connected) as a man of his station naturally would be. His wife Lenora, a heavy-set, blustery and determined southern lady with serious business acumen, ran a successful home-based business as a black market baby dealer.

She acquired babies from women in "unfortunate circumstances," assigned them a fair market price, and subsequently sold them to a waiting set of joyous new parents. The way she explained it was that she was performing a good deed for all concerned. Young unwed mothers were aided in giving their babies a "better life," childless couples found their happily-ever-afters, and the babies received loving, stable care that was above and beyond anything they might have expected in a single parent home. Most of the time it was assumed that the children would grow up never knowing the difference. One closed adoption; three happy, satisfied parties; and one humble little southern woman making it all come together.

This is the rosy picture of "closed" adoption that has taken root in the American psyche. It's a picture that birth mothers cling to when making the difficult decision to relinquish. It's a picture that helps adoptive parents breathe easy at night while their new infant sleeps close by. But in reality, the modern closed adoption process is a social aberration that has come under serious fire from many of its "beneficiaries."

The closed-adoption system also provided an opportunity for black market baby sellers to flourish in the United States and Canada during the mid-1900's. Blind spots and inefficiencies in the legal process, repressive social pressures on women, and an insatiable market demand all led to thousands of adoptions that were never legally documented or finalized. These factors are directly responsible for how I came to grow up in a woefully unfit home that I was destined to escape--physically at the age of sixteen, and legally at the age of forty-seven—when I sat before a judge in Florida and demanded justice from a system that had previously failed me at every step.

Chapter 1

I was born in 1952 in Jacksonville Florida, and at eight days old I went home with my new father, Alex Chalek, just after his illegally hired baby broker had passed over a sum of $200 to the attending physician at St. Luke's Hospital to cover my hospital stay.

Alex, or Al as he was mostly known, flashed a proud grin at Dr. R. A. Schnauss, an ophthalmologist of all things, and informed the good doctor that my name was Michael: Michael Edward Chalek, to be precise. Al accepted the obligatory congratulations and then bundled me off into the waiting car. Once at home, I was consigned to the care of his wife Adela, who fussed and made over me just as any first-time mother might. When it was clear within the first weeks at home that I had a bit of a virus coming on, she called a neighbor for advice and comfort. Together, the Chaleks and I embarked on the long journey of getting to know one another and of adapting to life as a family. Everything seemed picturesque.

For two-and-a-half years I was apparently quite the little prince of the castle. I grew strong and healthy and, most of all, insatiably curious about the world

1

around me. I loved to watch how things worked, and take them apart if possible (a common ailment of young boys). I was a small child who ate little and thought much. I knew nothing of adoption, or of my parents' ongoing attempts to have a child of their own.

On the day that my younger brother, Glenn, came home from the hospital, I was too young still to develop any permanent memory of the event. So what came on was a gradual understanding that I had changed somehow upon becoming a big brother. I was no longer as lovable, intelligent, capable or good as I had previously been. Unwilling to accept this in myself, I spent the next fourteen years hell bent on self-improvement.

The proof of my miserable failure wasn't evident in my school grades, which were excellent, or in my athletic abilities, where I starred on the track team, or even in my civic involvements, when I earned my Eagle Scout badge at the age of thirteen.

No, the proof was in my mother's eyes, and in her voice, and in the ever present switch that counted my failures out upon my skin. Once when I was four years old, she couldn't get a switch in her hands fast enough. So she beat me with the vacuum hose instead since she was busy cleaning house at the time of my infraction.

"Boots," Al would say, calling her by her nick-name. "Boots, I can't figure what that boy has done to rile you up. You sure don't go after Glenn that way."

Adela would raise an eyebrow, send me off to my room, and hustle Glenn off to her own bed, where he slept by her side until he was nearly a teenager.

Now since Al was a traveling salesman and gone on the road more than he was home, it might have been the case that my miserable relationship with my mother would have been vastly improved by a simple change in my father's career. But even when Al was home, his remarks on her treatment of me were motivated by mild curiosity rather than outrage. Not once did he intervene on my behalf. He watched as she beat me, or, if it suited him better, he took himself and his thoughts to another room.

Lying in my bed at night, I could hear the adults rambling through the house during the frequent dinner parties my parents held. Sometimes I would scoot to the door and press my ear to it, listening to the threads of conversation which carried through. Adela, during those times, shone in full and glorious beauty. Because she was beautiful, when Al was home and company was over and the world was good to her. She curled her hair, put on makeup and she dialed on the laughter and charm until every man in the room wished she were his.

Often the men would pass by my door, leaving the women in the kitchen or living room, and it was on one of these occasions that Al casually admitted the truth of my mother's feelings toward me and his own detachment to the matter. I don't know how the conversation began, nor where it ended, but I heard these few words loud and clear:

"God, no, Boots can't stand the boy. She's after him every second of the day," he said with a laugh.

A few deep chuckles and a couple of footsteps and the men were gone. I sat on the floor for a long while after, but my ear was no longer pressed against the door. My heart was breaking, but I refused to shed a single tear. Finally I crawled back into bed and covered my head with the pillow, shutting out any other random comments that might try to invade the bedroom which was my only sanctuary.

When the parties ended, Al would once again hit the road with his briefcase and his salesman's smile. Boots would take off the makeup and the pretty clothes, while the house descended into drudgery and silence and loneliness, at least for as long as I could manage to stay out of my mother's sight.

Glenn, who might have been a companion for me, became instead a minefield of potential infractions. When he was very young, it was generally unfortunate happenstance that would cause Adela's anger to rain down upon me, such as the fact of me being in the same room as Glenn when he began crying. But as we grew older, Glenn developed a delight in running and tattling so that he could watch our mother chase after me with the willow switch. When the beatings were over he would follow her out of the room, leaving me alone in my angry and resentful confusion. It became my habit to hide from Glenn and Adela both by retreating to my bedroom for the majority of the day.

Once, when I was six, I suffered a lapse in attentiveness to my mother's mood. It was a lesson I would never forget.

As usual, I was trying to figure out how something worked. This time it was one of my toy trucks, a masterful piece of machinery with actual working suspension. I was running it across the floor when I discovered that as the truck passed over the joiner between the living room carpet and the kitchen tile, the wheels would bounce up into their wells, absorbing the shock. Delighted, I decided to add extra weight to the bed of the truck by hauling some cargo. The cargo turned out to be another one of my toys. Lost in fascination, I ran the truck back and forth, back and forth, determined to understand.

Boots was not as charmed by the truck's inner workings as I was. Before I could react, she leapt from her seat at the table and hurtled toward me.

"If that's all the more you care about your toys," she said, "then let me just finish breaking them for you and get it over with."

With that, she brought up her foot and stomped it violently back down, crushing the truck and cracking the cab from the bed.

She returned to her seat at the table, and I gathered up my toys. With tears in my eyes, I fled to my room where I held my shattered truck to my chest and cried quietly into my sleeve.

Mike with adoptive parents
Circa 1953

Adela was not well suited to life as a salesman's wife. She had no driver's license, little education, and an extreme distaste of going into public without Al accompanying her. If we needed groceries while he was gone, the neighbor came and drove us into town. If we had an appointment to keep, the neighbor was there to help out again.

During these times, Glenn became a focus for all of Boots' restlessness. She mothered him with desperate attention: bathing him, feeding him, sleeping next to him, and all behind closed doors whenever possible so as to shut out any intrusion I might make onto the relationship. When her moods slipped into darker places, that's when she sought me out, switch in hand, wearing out the fit of temper on my back, buttocks and slender legs. When she was done, I was once again left alone.

As I entered school, I was thrilled to find a place where I could escape, and more importantly, a place where effort and ability was equated with predictable reward. My teachers, for sure, found my restless energy and inquisitive nature a bit of a burden in a school environment where children were expected to look straight ahead, answer only in turn and work in consistently focused silence. Until I entered seventh grade, all of my teachers passed me by in an unremarkable parade of tightly pinned hair, tightly pinched expressions and tight-lipped remonstrances to sit still and pay attention. And yet every report card went home with the highest grades.

Despite the pervasive signs of a child with a very troubled home life, the don't-ask, don't-tell deeply southern mentality of the 1950's kept teachers and school officials from making any inquiries. If the parents chose not to attend any of a student's sporting events, awards nights, school plays or otherwise, that was none of anyone's business. If the student bore bruises and welts that occasionally made it into the light of day, the problem was easily solved by looking the other way.

That is, until the year that Eleanor Berger came to town. Mrs. Berger, the school's new seventh grade teacher, was a *northerner* of all things. Twenty-one years old, progressive and strong willed, it's a wonder she was ever hired at all. She brought with her strong liberal notions that were vastly outside of the box, especially in the deeply conservative south. She shocked the educational community by introducing *sex education* as part of the curriculum in her classroom, an unprecedented move in 1965, at least outside of her home state of New York.

But hired she was, and she entered my life like a breath of fresh air. It was during that seventh grade year that I began to truly hate the South and the closed minded, secretive culture which had evolved there. Elle Berger came in, clear eyed and curious and enthusiastic and, in one year, changed the course my life was destined to take.

Mostly, what she offered me was simply encouragement and support. When Mrs. Berger looked at me, she truly *looked* at me. When I was out of line, she let me know. But when I excelled, or showed particular skill, she was also generous with her praise.

She refused to accept that my parents could be simply left out of the school equation like an unnecessary appendage. I don't know to this day how she did it, but she got Al and Adela Chalek into her classroom for a rare parent-teacher conference, attempting to ferret out of them the nature of my home life. When it was clear that she would make no inroads on that front, she became even more supportive of me, both in and out of the classroom.

I remember the day I earned the rank of Eagle Scout. It was extremely rare then for a scout so young to achieve the honor. Despite the hours of commitment I had made, and the importance of the event, I knew that neither of my parents would attend. So I invited the only other person whose opinion mattered to me. I asked Mrs. Berger if she would come to the ceremony.

"I'd be honored, Michael," she responded.

So on that evening, when I walked off of the stage having received the ultimate scouting rank, it was my teacher's proud smile and shining eyes that greeted me, and whose memory I carried with me throughout the following long and lonely years—years in which despite my every effort, I could do no right, and Glenn could do no wrong.

*   *   *   *   *   *

It bears mentioning that by the time I was ending

my elementary years, I had managed to both infuriate my mother and marginally shut her down, by ferociously denying her final attempt to bathe me when I fell extremely ill at the age of nine with an illness known as Bright's disease. It was an illness that attacked my liver and kept me bedridden for eight full weeks of third grade.

Although she did not attempt to "help" me in this way as frequently as she did Glenn, on occasion throughout my middle childhood she would accompany me into the bathroom at night. Without dwelling on the details, her assistance was of a type that left me feeling ashamed and violated.

I tried several times to let my father know how I felt about these instances. His response was always harsh and dismissive.

"Your mother has never shown you anything but loving care," he told me. "Your ungratefulness is disgusting."

Despite my sheltered and repressed childhood, my awareness grew that it was inappropriate in the extreme for my mother to be running her hands along my body, up into my crotch, lingering with the soaping and scrubbing as she did so. On that day when I was nine, I decided I'd had enough. I was feverish, and miserable, but not so far gone that I couldn't fight her off. This time I was old enough and strong enough to make it clear that she might get away with beating me and verbally abusing me, but never again would she touch me in *that* way.

I think that her attempt was partly motivated by several fights that took place over those eight weeks. My third grade teacher, Mrs. Betsy Jenkins, had graciously taken it upon herself to nightly tutor me after school to keep my academic progress on track. I looked forward to her visits with joyous anticipation.

My delight was a thorn in Adela's side. She mentioned several times, in angry outbursts, that I was a horrible child for loving another woman more than I loved my own mother. She accused me of being ungrateful and cruel.

In the midst of all of this, Adela lost the will to maintain the family "secret" any longer. Looking back, I think she must have been waiting for the opportunity to let me know of my adoption, and that somehow Alex had prevented it.

One day, I unwittingly opened the door for her. It was on a warm fall afternoon shortly after my illness. I had dared to take a rare break from the confines of my room. Oil painting was my newest hobby and the natural light was much better in the kitchen. Adela was also in the kitchen, standing at the sink peeling potatoes. While I was painting, I started talking to her.

One of my classmates at school had just revealed to us that he was adopted. The concept was a new one to me. I knew almost nothing about adoption, and new topics and concepts were a challenge I rarely turned away.

So I told my mother what was on my mind. Tilting my head at the numbered canvas, brush in hand, I mentioned to her what I had learned.

"There's a kid in my class today who told us that he's adopted," I said.

"Hmm," Adela replied, without turning around. "Well, you know that you're adopted, too."

With no preparation, no backward glance, she dropped this bomb into the empty conversational space. She continued to peel and slice and stare out the window, the metallic scrape of the knife now the only sound in the room. What she was thinking at the moment, I can only guess.

I, however, was dumbstruck. The paintbrush shook in my hands. I no longer saw the canvas, or the kitchen, or my mother. The rest of the evening disappeared into the shadows while I wrestled with the implications.

When my father returned later in the week, I confronted him in the hallway. He still had on his hat and coat, and his briefcase had just been settled at the door.

"Mom says I'm adopted," I told him.

"That's true," he responded. "We adopted you when you were an infant."

There didn't seem much else to say.

Once the secret was out, Adela delighted in mentioning my adopted status at regular intervals. It became another way for her to abuse me, lashing out verbally with results as painful as any physical beating.

By the end of that school year, I had developed a pronounced stutter that would follow me for the rest of my life. It certainly did nothing to endear me to my already critical parents. And while many experts debate the exact causes of speech disorders such as mine, I have no doubt that it was induced by a type of post-traumatic stress disorder brought on by the constant verbal abuse that Adela dealt out to me.

Mike at three years old
with Adela and younger brother
Glenn
1955

Chapter 2

When I was in high school, Alex took a job in the Chicago area. He was originally from Illinois, so it was a natural place for us to relocate. The move to Illinois was another empowering factor in the eventual course of my life, although I didn't realize it until much later. At this point I was starting to throw myself into sports, running on the track team with great success.

While Adela's power somewhat waned over my life as I became a teenager, Al's grew in strength and intensity. In Chicago, his new job put him more frequently at home. And where Adela's force had been oppositional and violent, Al was simply an impenetrable wall around me whose boundaries grew ever more confined.

Alex Chalek was a trim, athletic, handsome and supremely self-controlled former soldier who couldn't let go of his militaristic concepts of authority and discipline. He was not a tall man, but he chose to focus on pursuits that required no significant height advantages. He was an excellent golfer, a master at chess, a mean poker player, and one hell of an authoritarian at home with his wife and children. I always thought that one day, with my excellent grades and my continued success in sports and civics, Al would finally discover a reason to be proud of me, since success was a trait he valued highly. The wished-for approval never happened.

Instead, except for when I was at school and sports practice I was treated like a juvenile delinquent. Without any provocation, the family decided I wasn't to be allowed out of the house unsupervised. Whereas my fellow classmates were stretching their wings, borrowing the family car, going on dates and to school dances, I was banned from all such activity. It was not unusual for Al and Adela to leave the house on their own date and still hire a babysitter for me and Glenn. By the time I was in high school, the babysitter's presence was an obvious slap in the face. And then, at the end of my eleventh grade year, Al also went to my track coach and convinced the man to cut me from the team. I don't know how or why, he just did it.

For the junior prom, I was given rare permission to attend the dance and was even promised the use of my otherwise neglected driver's license. I was to be allowed to drive myself and my date, unsupervised. By the time the night arrived, Al had changed his mind. We rode to the school with him chauffeuring us and me climbing miserably out of the backseat in full view of my classmates. Al drove off with a loud warning to be ready for pick-up at curfew. I ducked my head in shame as we passed by the other students.

When I objected to the tight reins that Al kept on

the household, and on me particularly, he would draw himself up to his full (although meager) height and let me know that if it were *his* strict Russian immigrant father raising me, I'd find myself kneeling on dried rice or beans for hours while I learned to repent of my rebellious ways. Instead, I was lucky to be treated as lovingly as I was.

"After all," Adela would here interject. "Didn't we buy and pay enough for you? Show a little more respect." Sometimes, she would mention that their money could have been better spent on more rounds of artificial insemination. Then Glenn might have had a biological sibling instead of just me.

Here their eyes would meet, briefly, and Al would return to his dinner, or his paper. And I would return to my good soldier routine, with answers of "Yes, sir" and "No, sir" and I would bury myself in studying for the extra classes I was taking throughout my high school semesters and summer terms. While I studied, Al and Adela would fret over Glenn's failing grades and whether he might be held back again. The marked difference between my school performance and Glenn's did nothing to improve my relationship with either my brother or our parents.

When we arrived in Chicago, I got my first look at my own birth certificate—the amended one standardly issued for all adoptees—and noticed a discrepancy that sparked a question I immediately regretted asking.

Adela pulled out the certificate and gave it to me so that I could go in and register for classes at my new high school. I looked over the document, and asked about why June 1953 was listed as the day the document was registered, over a year after I was born.

Her reaction was instantaneous, defensive and cruel. Instead of answering my question, she said," You know, if I could ram you back up in your mother's womb I would do it." I decided then and there that I would never ask her again about anything pertaining to my birth.

Instead, the extra classes I took during high school became central to a new plan for emotional survival. Since school was the one thing I was allowed to pursue without hindrance, I pursued it with every spare moment of my time. By the end of eleventh grade I had only one class left to graduate.

In addition to dedicating myself to this accelerated schedule, I had also found a way, despite the clear obstacles, to sneak in a steady relationship with a girlfriend several years older than I was. Her name was Susan. She had an apartment in Wheaton, a town about thirty miles away from where I lived. Together we planned for me to enact a grand escape. I finished my last credits in the summer term of 1969, and in August I received my diploma.

That same week, after months of premeditation, it was simply time to leave. I grabbed a hidden suitcase from under the bed, shoved in as many clothes as it would hold, grabbed a few papers and my ID, and crawled out the window. I left the sleeping household behind, never to return. For the next five months I was a seventeen-year-old fugitive, lying low in Susan's apartment and biding my time until the day I turned eighteen. To my knowledge, the Chaleks never sought me out. But I wasn't taking any chances. I kept a constant eye out for notices in the paper and I avoided all sightings of the police.

* * * * * *

Mike at 16 years old
Circa 1968

If there was one thing life had taught me up to this point, it was that academic pursuit was the path to success. So, although jobs were plentiful in Chicago in the 70s—really, all you had to do was walk into the plant and say "I want to work"—I decided to go to college. A year of hard labor in the factories had convinced me that it wasn't the future I desired.

I had taken the ACT and SAT in high school, with good results, and those scores plus my high school GPA easily gained me acceptance into the University of Illinois. I started living on campus during the week, traveling home to be with Susan on the weekends.

By my final year of college, Susan and I were married. Instead of being a wonderful new beginning, though, it was more of a final death knell for our relationship. It's the mark of many years of distance and gained wisdom that I can look back and say that my previous experience of "family" had ill prepared me to be the husband that Susan wanted.

I didn't know what a strong, healthy, intimate adult relationship should look like. I certainly hadn't been taught that at home. Susan needed an emotional connection. She wanted children. Her vision of marriage and the reality of what I could offer were so far apart that it drove us both to distraction. She started drinking. A year later, I left.

After my bachelor's degree was completed, it seemed natural to think about going to grad school. I was certainly comfortable as a student. It was one of the few things at which I had always excelled. So eventually, I found myself back in the classroom, working and studying just like always, leaving little time to think about life, failed families or loneliness.

Sometimes I would call Glenn. Especially after I turned eighteen, I couldn't help the curiosity of wanting to know how things were going, if anyone missed me, where they all were. Eventually, in 1973, Glenn and the family moved back to Florida. I lost touch even with him. I never once spoke to Al or Adela.

I had one cousin, too, that I called regularly. His name was Joe. He was a good twelve years older than I, and he was included in the adult circles at family events and holidays. He was a much more regular and reliable source of information than Glenn, even though Joe was married and in the process of pursuing a career. In fact, in 1977 he invited me to spend the holidays with him and his wife. He made the mistake of telling Alex and Adela, however, and Adela proceeded to object vehemently. She told him that I was a bore and would do nothing but ruin the entire holiday for them.

Despite the seeming isolation I endured, what ultimately happened was that the 1970s nearly passed me by. Before I knew it, I had successfully completed two degrees and was happily remarried. Then one day, in 1979, the earth shifted beneath my feet and I realized that I was not content with the limbo where I was existing between two worlds. I had no ties to the family that raised me, and I had no knowledge of the family that had given me life. It was time for things to change.

The precipitating event was this: I had become a father. In 1979 my first son was born. I was thrilled. It's a moment like no other. I held the celebratory cigar in my hands and looked at it and thought, *there is no one for me to call*. My son had no grandparents on my side to spoil him, or to cheer his growth. Now it was not just my own family line that was broken off, but it was this child's as well. And that was a thought I didn't lightly bear.

I did call Joe, of course, even though we talked less frequently now. I told him of my son's birth and my unpleasant lines of thought on the matter of family, and he confirmed what I already knew.

"Aunt Boots?" he said. "No, she doesn't have any interest in you at all. Glenn is the only thing ever on her mind."

It was hardly surprising. But it did surprise me that the words fell like more strokes of the switch against my skin.

* * * * * *

For almost fifteen long years, my efforts to discover something about my birth family would go completely fruitless. But no matter how many times I met with a dead end, I always found myself trying *one more time* to see if a new avenue had opened up.

In 1980, searching for a birth mother in a closed adoption triad was a vastly different experience from searching today. There were no email lists, internet support groups, online genealogical archives or digitized documents. Instead, if you were lucky enough to live in a larger city, what you had were actual in-person support groups that met frequently to share resources and ideas. If you had money, there were private investigators who would work on your behalf and who advertised through the search and reunion groups.

Generally, though, for anyone to successfully help you with a search, whether a support group volunteer or a paid private investigator, you needed a starting place—a crucial piece of information that assisted you in moving the search forward. For me, that starting place was a long ways off. I began learning about the difficult path ahead by making some new friends at one of these adoption reunion groups in Chicago. The group was known as *Truth Seekers in Adoption* and is still running strong today. I started attending their weekly meetings. And I began following some of their suggestions.

I quickly exhausted all of the normally recommended search methods. You see, while above-board and *legally finalized* adoptions are supposed to follow a rather predictable schedule, many US adoptions are tied up with an underlying deception of one sort or another. In the meetings in Chicago, I met individuals from every part of the adoption triad: birth parents, adoptees, and even adoptive parents. I was shocked by the ways in which many of these individuals shared how the adoption process had been bent, broken and circumvented in the early-to-mid 1900s.

For instance, many birth mothers revealed that they were pressured, against their will, to relinquish babies whom they desperately desired to raise themselves. Most of these were women who were unwed at the time of their pregnancies. Some were sent by family members to be held captive in so-called Maternity Homes, not to be allowed a return until the baby had been born and relinquished. Without a societal support system for single mothers, 80% of US infants born to them from the 1940s up until the 1970s were given over to the adoption system (as opposed to fewer than 4% relinquishments by 1983). The adoption system, at the time of these record high relinquishments, was almost exclusively closed— meaning the original birth certificates would never be seen by the adult adoptees, and the child's future status, development and accomplishments would never be known to the mother, a fit punishment for her sins.

These mothers I met who were involved in the search movement have never lost their deep, primal need to know that their children were safe and well, and to know if that child endured a burning need of his own to discover the missing pieces of his biological history. Unfortunately compounding the search and reunion efforts, many of the so-called adoptions of the 1950s and 1960s were little more than black market transactions facilitated by the maternity homes, the hospitals or the delivering physician. In these cases, a completely fraudulent original birth certificate would have been forged with the adoptive mother listed as the actual biological mother, effectively rendering the true birth mother a non-entity and any future reunion attempts completely hopeless. Frequently the birth mother was unaware that the legal adoption process had never taken place.

Hard to believe? In the current era of information hyperabundance it takes no more than a quick internet search for the term "Cole babies" to introduce you to the existence of such black market baby rings and their prevalence in the US during the mid-20th century.

Other methods of circumventing the adoption system also thrived in the atmosphere of legal and social suppression that unmarried women faced in those days. Frequently the infant would be "abducted" by distant family members from out of state, with the blessing of the maternal grandparents, and no involvement of any lawyers or state agencies.

In some small towns and counties, courts would push through questionable adoption documents and arrangements for reasons related to the social connections of the adoptive parents or the baby broker. Especially when an infant was procured out of state or out of town, falsified names or forged signatures on relinquishments would be difficult to prove if an unscrupulous lawyer, doctor or public notary was involved. It was easier just to sign the adoption decree and let everyone move forward.

Despite the fact that I met many reunion seekers who had discovered some sort of fraudulent activity in their own adoptions, I had no idea at the time that my own adoption was anything less than legal and above-board. I had a copy of my amended birth certificate that listed the Chaleks as my legal parents. I hired a private detective in Florida (the first of many) to look up my adoption record in Gainesville, in Alachua County. Everything seemed in order, but the details were, of course, sealed.

Another step I took was to write to the state of Florida, at the Department of Health and Rehabilitative Services (HRS) and request non-identifying information on my birth family. This was a legal remedy created to give adoptees access to any pertinent medical information that case workers discovered during the adoption process through interviews with the birth mother. The closed adoption files are kept by a custodian, who interprets and releases the non-identifying information upon proof that it is the actual adoptee who is requesting it.

This first request I made for non-identifying information resulted in the shortest imaginable letter of response, with details that proved almost useless to my efforts except to say that my birth mother was young and healthy and reported nothing that indicated any genetically related conditions on either side of the family. Despite this obvious dead-end, I wasn't yet deterred in my first search effort. I called the hospital listed on my birth certificate and had the first lucky break of many over the next two decades. Somehow I convinced the medical records clerk at the hospital to search through the names of all the women who had delivered a white male infant in that hospital on the date of January 25, 1952. There were five. Only one of them did not have a last name that matched the listed birth father's.

This woman, who was listed as Faye Barnwell, matched the last name on file for adoption of a Baby Boy Barnwell that the private detective had located in his search of the public records. I felt confident that this, then, was my birth mother. She was listed as sixteen years old. Her name plus the identity of a caseworker named Mrs. Fielding were all the further information I could glean from the records department.

I wish I had known then what a false trail was ahead of me based on the information this helpful records clerk had provided. Let me make it clear that, even then, it was highly unlikely that a hospital employee would provide this type of information due to rules and regulations governing personal medical records. In the current era of HIPAA privacy laws, it would be downright impossible to obtain anything in a similar manner.

* * * * * *

Armed with the names of Faye Barnwell, Mrs. Fielding, and Dr. R. A. Schnauss (the ophthalmologist who had delivered me), I began an earnest attempt to contact any one of these individuals in an effort to further my search. I spent even more money on private investigators and on long-distance phone calls. In the end, I met with nothing but disappointment.

Many of the pitfalls I encountered had to do with the booming search and reunion business that was opening up in the US at this time, as more and more adoptees discovered through family rumor or buried legal papers or simple intuition, that they were not natural born members of their families. To the surprise and discomfort of an entire system, many of the adoptees, no matter how wonderful their adoptive homes might have been, were not content with the answer that their own biological history was none of their legal business. The once powerless infants had grown up and were now full rights-holding, free-thinking citizens of the world's premier democracy. These adoptees were demanding access to their own genetic information for a myriad of valid personal reasons. And since the US government was not providing fast enough recognition of the adoptees' legal claims and their demands for information, plenty of businesses sprang up to supply whatever information could be gleaned through alternative channels. It was unregulated capitalism at its finest.

In the end, some of the investigators and "experts" I hired were well meaning, and some of them were qualified, and few of them were both. In a span of three nearly wasted years I spent ungodly sums of money going down hopeless false trails, all in search of a woman named Faye Barnwell whom I assumed had given birth to me nearly thirty years earlier.

For the years between 1983 and 1988, nothing of any importance happened to further my quest. Then, in 1988, I made a brief trip to Jacksonville to try and do on my own the tasks the investigators had failed to accomplish.

During that trip, I went by the hospital from my amended birth certificate, and there I obtained a physical copy of my own hospital medical records. I tracked down a Dr. Schnauss, only to discover that he was not the man who had delivered me, but his son. This younger Dr. Schnauss informed me, furthermore, that all records from his father's medical practice had been destroyed several years prior. He had known nothing of the deliveries his father had been performing as a side business in the 1950s, especially since it was so removed from the typical services of an eye doctor.

As a final resort, I appealed to the Chief Judge of Alachua County, the Honorable Chester B. Chance, to inquire if there was any way I might expect some judicial assistance in my quest to reclaim my own personal information. The judge, of course, sent me packing. He informed me that if I seriously wanted to gain access to information about my biological identity, I would be better served by going down to Tallahassee and having a talk with the state legislators. The adoption record, as the law stood, was sealed. There was nothing he could do, even if he had wanted.

This last trip left me drained, financially and emotionally. For six years, the search stalled. Part of me suspected I might not see a change in adoptee rights in my lifetime. I grieved the loss, both for me and for my children and their own heritage.

Chapter 3

By the beginning of 1994 I was still frequently thinking about and grieving the loss of my biological identity, but without any legislative changes at a federal or state level granting me access to a copy of my original birth certificate, I was out of ideas and out of steam. I had returned to live in Florida for work and personal reasons, despite my deep dislike of the South. I kept myself busy with my career and children—two sons—and tried to ignore the gnawing hunger and anger that I felt whenever I dwelt on thoughts of closed adoptions, legal red-tape and a broken sense of self.

It was then that I received a certified letter in the mail from Glenn. Inside it was a copy of the last will and testament of Alex Chalek. Al had passed away on June 2, 1993 and made Glenn his personal representative. Over six months later, Glenn was in the process of wrapping up the legalities. At the last possible moment, I was informed of not only Al's death, but of my mention in the will and of the impending discharge of the estate.

I had not spoken to any of the Chaleks in years. I knew that Adela had preceded her husband in death, although I also heard about her passing many months after the fact. Al's death was a surprise, of sorts, mostly because I had so completely severed any personal connections that I no longer thought of myself as a part of my adoptive family. Receiving the will in the mail, knowing that I had been mentioned as one of Alex's heirs, I felt an odd sense of dislocation. For a moment, unwanted memories of childhood clouded my mind and prevented me from reading too deeply into the pages I clutched in my hands.

Sending these unhappy thoughts packing, I took the letter to a table and began to read. It was clear that the will would not take me long to decipher. It was comprised of only five legal-size pages, two of which were a handwritten codicil (addendum) published quite a few years after the original will. As I read through the document and began to understand how it related to me, I was beset by both sadness and rage at the final blow my adoptive father had dealt me from beyond the grave.

The original last will and testament of Al D. Chalek was a three page typewritten document that was compiled and signed in November of 1982. At that point in time, I would have been 30 years old and well out of the Chaleks' lives by my own choice. It made sense, then, painful as it seemed, that Al had failed to mention me in the will at all. He designated Adela as his primary beneficiary and personal representative, with Glenn as a secondary should Adela not survive her husband.

Again, although it was a painful reminder of my

non-existent family ties, the original will could and should have been nothing more than a closing chapter to a very sad story.

Instead, attached to the original filing was the two page handwritten codicil, dated in 1988, which served the purpose of adding one small paragraph to the original document.

The Codicil stated (in part):

> *This Codicil is to demonstrate that I had not overlooked my adopted son, Michael Edward Chalek. Article II "Distribution" is amended by adding the following paragraph C.*
> *C. In the event my spouse, Adela, does not survive me, then I devise the sum of One Dollar ($1.00) to my adopted son, Michael Edward Chalek, in that he is self-supporting and for other good reasons known to all of us.*

In a few sentences, Al had uncovered and bloodied all of an adoptee's most vulnerable places. First, I had been left out of the original will altogether, without a single mention. Glenn was their son, their *only* son. Painful, but not surprising.

Second, Al followed up that document by making clear that the only reason he was amending the will was to "demonstrate" that he hadn't overlooked me, a term which implies a possibility of an accidental omission. In short, he was saying "I did it on purpose." Now his only reason to mention me at all was to protect the original document from any legal claims against its validity. Summarized further, the statement was indicative of the fact that they were being forced to acknowledge my legal standing as their child and that they felt their "real" son needed protection from me in case I wanted to take away any of his inheritance.

Third, Al referred to me, not once, but twice as his "adopted" son. Adoptees, regardless of their situations, generally tend to have some level of fear that this second-class status is how their parents view them. Fair? No. Real? Yes.

Finally, there was the question of the statement Al made about "other good reasons known to all of us."

I can't tell you how long I sat and stared and pondered over that eight word phrase. From my view, what I had done for the Chaleks was to survive their neglect and abuse for seventeen years, and then do them the favor of disappearing from their lives forever without a single demand for recompense or explanation. What was this inference on Al's part that I had been the one to commit a wrong that was deserving of punishment?

As my mind connected the dots, starting with the dates of the two documents, the wording of the codicil, and the fact that I was receiving all of the correspondence at the last possible hour before final discharge of the estate—another indication that my motives were under suspicion—a long denied fury at the injustice of the entire situation began to burn within me.

I wondered, who were these people? Why had they adopted a child, and how had they managed to convince the system to grant them one? These questions were not going to disappear, and I added them to the list of many others I had regarding my legal and biological histories.

*   *   *   *   *   *

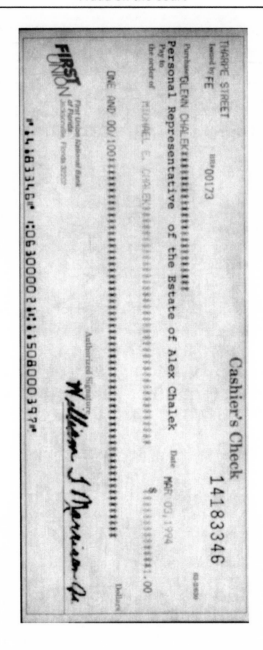

Glenn himself did nothing to improve matters when I finally reached out to him about a subject that had long bothered me. In short, I had spent many years wishing that I could retrieve my personal belongings that had remained behind when I crawled out that bedroom window. I decided it was time to make my request known before a thorough cleaning of the attic took place and any chance I had was gone forever.

By the time I called Glenn to ask about my school records and awards, the matter of the will had been quickly dispatched. In the spring of 1994 I received a cashier's check from Al's estate, in the amount of one dollar. The check was dated March 03, 1994 and listed Glenn as the purchaser. I variously debated shredding, filing, burning or displaying it, until finally I put it in a frame and hung it on my office wall.

Glenn and I clearly did not consider ourselves brothers in any sense of the term. But I hoped that in the spirit of human decency, he might be persuaded to forward the small number of personal records that I hoped still existed from my childhood. I'd worked hard for the grades and the accolades (including my Eagle Scout award), and I had children whose baby pictures I'd enjoy comparing with my own. With these goals in mind, I picked up the phone and made a wish for luck.

"Hey Glenn," I said when he answered. "It's Mike."

"Mike..." Glenn replied warily. "What do you want?"

"Thought I would touch base," I said. "And ask about something that's been on my mind. I've been wondering if we could arrange a way for me to get back some of my personal belongings, stuff from when I was a kid, you know?"

Glenn let out a huff of breath.

"I don't know if any of that stuff is still around," he said.

"Could you check? I just want school records, anything from the scouts, the awards from the track team. I'd guess Adela would have kept it all in one place."

"I suppose I can give it a look when I have time," Glenn finally replied.

"I'd appreciate it. Need my address?" I asked.

"No, I've got it from Dad's will," he said.

"Ok, well thanks. I really would love to have those things back."

"Sure," Glenn replied.

The conversation had clearly reached its end for us both. We said goodbye.

I never received the items, or any other contact from Glenn. He moved, changed numbers, and as far as I can tell has made every effort to ensure I never locate him again. None of his few living relatives know of his whereabouts, or will admit to it.

I made one other significant call as a result of Al's passing and my receipt of the will. The call was to Al's brother, Bill Chalek. Although Bill's name showed up nowhere in the legal documentation, I knew he had been the one responsible for supplying the advice and terminology that resulted in Al's amendment to the will.

Colonel William "Bill" Chalek was none other than

the successful, highly decorated and powerfully connected war hero and former POW who was known for having authored a memoir of his own experiences as a captured fighter pilot in WWII. He retired from the military after some 28 years and then opened up a private practice law firm in Florida. Al wouldn't have filed a single document without first running it by his big brother, the lawyer.

I couldn't get the question out of my mind as to what Al had meant by the mean-spirited and rather obtuse reference to "all good reasons" in his justification of my $1.00 inheritance. If anyone could tell me, it was my good old uncle Bill. Whether he *would* tell me was highly doubtful, but as I was now in a habit of pursuing every open avenue to its furthest end, I made the call.

"Colonel," I said when I reached him at his home.

"Who's this?" he asked.

"It's Mike Chalek," I answered. "Al's adopted son."

"What in God's name do you want now? You got your dollar didn't you?"

I resisted, for the time, engaging in a battle of tempers. I needed to know what only he could tell me.

"I don't want money," I replied.

"Then what is it?"

"I just wanted to know about Al's will, about the sentence you put in there that says he had all good reasons to leave me that dollar, and that everyone knew them."

Bill wasn't pulled in by the bait.

"I didn't write that will, Mike. Al did that all on his own."

"Bull crap," I replied. "And I'll tell you, whatever that's meant to imply about me and my choices, I resent it. I haven't ever been the one who's behaved criminally, or stolen a thing from anyone. You want to know about that kind of thing, just take a look at their *real* son."

I was irritated enough to let Bill know that I had heard about Glenn's adult behavior and brushes with the law (including armed robbery). I hoped that by bringing his nephew up now I could rankle the old man just enough to get him talking about the Codicil and its meaning.

"What do you want, Mike? You want the truth, is that it?"

"Well Colonel, I think there's this assumption among your type that the rest of us, the general public, can't handle the truth. But I think that *you* are the one who can't handle it," I said.

Yes, I enjoyed myself and my little movie reference. It wasn't an accidental quote.

And, ridiculously, it worked.

"Alright," Bill said. "Alright."

He sighed.

"I did help your father, I mean Al, with the Codicil. But I just offered general advice," he said.

"He had to have told you what he meant by that, though," I objected. "I mean, it says right there...*known to all of us...* If you aren't included in that statement then who in the world is?"

"Mike, I'm telling you, I don't know. And I don't know who would."

* * * * * *

As 1994 ended and we celebrated the dawn of a new year, I was drawn once again into the world of adoption search and reunion. The Glenn/Bill/Al ordeal had lit a fire within me that, despite many future obstacles and delays, would never again fail to burn. More than ever, I was glad that I could say to the world that no Chalek blood actually ran through my veins. But that left me with nothing, no identity at all to fall back upon.

I spent much time during these intervening years in thinking about adoption procedures and the current legislative environment. I'd decided where I stood on a few important issues. One of those issues had to do with the suitability of adoptive families from a compatibility standpoint. I wondered if I could see into my adoption record, whether anyone responsible for my placement had looked at my birth parents and analyzed their interests, background, talent, intelligence and other personality traits and said, "Yes, this child might predictably be expected to fit well into the personality and lifestyle of his adoptive home."

I guess you could say that, in the debate of nature versus nurture, I was leaning toward saying "both" with a slight advantage to the genetic component.

How else could one explain the extreme disparity between my love of academic pursuit, learning, mathematics and engineering when compared to the interests of the people who raised me? Neither of my adoptive parents were highly educated, they were aggressively anti-religious (I found absolutely no guidance in seeking to understand my beliefs on deity or spirituality), and no matter how much I tried, I could not connect with any of the three other members of my family. There was a clearly marked difference between *me*, and *them*.

Some of these thoughts were also responsible for driving me back to my quest to reunite with my birth family. Since I was nothing like my adoptive family (the nurture side of the equation), was I anything like my biological one?

It was a good time to be getting back into the business of searching. In 1995 a new tool appeared that would connect me to an unprecedented number of other adoptees, with equally unprecedented information sharing and access. In other words, I received a free trial of AOL.

Anyone who owned a postal address during the heyday of AOL will remember the cardboard CD cases that showed up almost monthly, begging you to install their software and find out just how wonderful cyberspace could be. Jokes abounded on late night television about the discs and the various possible uses that might be made of them, or about the strain they were placing on landfills nationwide.

I took that first disc I received and immediately popped it into my computer. I'm a software engineer. I couldn't help myself.

Within a few hours of use of that thirty day trial, I made one of the first major strides in reopening my search. I joined some genealogy related web rings, hoping to dig up more on any families in Florida with the last name of Barnwell. It was still the only name I had to work with, and my hope was that my birth mother was actually from the area and hadn't been shipped there from out of state (I also believed at the time that she was only 16 when she had given birth to me).

I can't now recall exactly how it happened, but in one of those online chat rooms I met a man named Doug Diamond. He was also an adoptee from Florida who had searched for—and found—his birth mother. As we chatted about my own efforts to date and what I knew, he expressed incredulity at the amount of information I had wrung out of the hospital records department. When I brought up the name of Mrs. Fielding (the caseworker listed in my hospital records) it sparked a new intensity in Doug's responses.

"I know Mrs. Fielding," he wrote. "At least if it's the same woman who was involved in my own adoption."

"What?" I typed.

"Yeah. She was a famous baby broker in the area during the 1950's. She brokered my adoption. And quite a few others under the table."

I stared at the screen, perplexed. I hadn't seen

anything in my search so far that led me to believe I had been a party to that type of transaction. My adoption was legally finalized, my birth certificate amended. A judge had signed off on all of it.

"How did that work?" I asked.

"Mrs. Fielding, Lenora was her name, enticed young unwed mothers into her home, kept them as boarders until they gave birth. Then she sold the babies to waiting couples," Doug explained.

I was incensed. No wonder Al and Adela had always referred to "purchasing" me.

"I got in touch with Mrs. Fielding's daughter a few years ago," Doug continued.

"What happened?" I asked.

"She confirmed that she remembered how her mother had kept pregnant women in their home when she was growing up. I guess we're not the first people to go looking for information. She said that as far as she knows, the records are gone. She checked with her sister, too."

"So there's no help for me there," I said.

"You know what you need to do?" asked Doug. "Write to the reunion registry people again. There's a new woman in charge up there, and she seems to be much more sympathetic to the adoptees."

"What would be the point of that?" I asked.

"You never know. She might put something more into *her* letter. Something you could use to get going again."

Despite my reservations, I did just that. I sent off

a new request to the adoption reunion registry, complete with a copy of my driver's license as required. I didn't hold out much hope, but you can't ever prevent a tiny little flame from kindling with every new attempt.

While I waited for a response, Doug agreed to do a few little inquiries of his own into the matter. He lived in the Jacksonville area and because of his adoption experience, he was just as diligent and persistent as I could have been myself. He made copies of contact info for anyone with a last name of Barnwell in the local directories who were also listed in 1951-1953 (yes, he went to the directory archives for me). Despite his generous assistance, the research led nowhere.

My letter requesting information was sent on July 20, 1995. The response was dated August 15th of the same year. The difference between the response from Mrs. Marquess and the letter from her predecessor was nearly comical. My new letter of non-identifying information was a full five-pages long. I flipped quickly through the pages just to get an idea, then began reading.

A few things popped out at me immediately, some phrases I marked for review later:

> *When you were born, your birth mother was 22 years old. She was married, but had been separated from her husband for four years...Therefore, your birth mother's husband, your legal, but not your natural father did have to give his consent for your adoption.*

While all of this info was contradictory to what I had received from the hospital, it did not cause anywhere near the stomach-clenching frustration I experienced when I read the next paragraphs.

> *Your birth mother signed her Consent for your adoption...using an assumed name. [but] the consent was allowed to stand.*
>
> *Your adoption was arranged by an Adoption Broker by the name of Mrs. Fielding who operated in Jacksonville at the time of your birth. This woman was particularly uncooperative with the State Welfare case worker and it took several weeks for the case worker to locate your birth mother after the Chalek family filed their petition to adopt you. **The record indicates that it was this woman who advised your birth mother to enter the hospital under an assumed name and to also sign her Consent using an assumed name. The Broker told your birth mother that this was being done to assure her confidentiality** [emphasis added].*
>
> *Your birth mother was interviewed by the department case worker on September 9, 1952. Your birth mother **did ask the case worker if there was a chance you could be returned to her** [emphasis added]. In the record the worker stated that "It was difficult for*

the birth mother to discuss this situation at all as she manifested a great deal of feeling about having placed the baby and frankly stated that she could not discuss it at all without crying.

...

Your birth mother was unwilling to name your natural father in the case record...[she] related to the case worker that she had ended her relationship with your natural father. He did not know of the pregnancy, of your birth or that you had been placed for adoption...that your natural father had first told her he was unmarried. However, after the pregnancy occurred, your birth mother stated that she had found out that your natural father was in fact married, and was the father of two children.

...

In discussing the plans she had made for your adoption, your birth mother stated that she had told several of her girlfriends about her situation once she realized that she was pregnant with you. Your birth mother stated that it was during this time that she saw an advertisement in the local paper regarding persons who wanted to adopt and also release a child for adoption.

Your birth mother called the phone number and was eventually put in touch with the Adoption Broker. Your birth mother stated that after she talked with this woman she felt that she would be doing the best thing for both of you. Your birth mother stated that the woman told her that your adoptive parents would pay her doctor bills and her bill for the hospital.

Your birth mother stated that she stayed with her friends throughout the pregnancy and only contacted this Mrs. Fielding when she went into labor. Your birth mother stated that Mrs. Fielding had advised her not to see you after birth as this would be easier later on. Your birth mother stated that this had not been the case and she had continuously worried how you were getting along.

...

[She] further explained that she had wanted to register your birth in either her married name or in her maiden name. However she stated that Mrs. Fielding would not allow this and thus your birth was registered in a purely fictitious name. As far as I can determine, though the matter was cleared up for the court, <u>there was never</u>

> *any effort undertaken to correct your*
> *original birth certificate to show the*
> *correct information. The Adoption [sic]*
> *told your birth mother that by continuing*
> *this ruse, no one would ever know that*
> *she had given birth to you or had placed*
> *you for adoption.*

I needn't mention that by this point, not only was my gut clenching, but my blood beginning to boil. I was being talked about, and bartered, like an art print or a collector's item. My birth mother, who wanted to do the right thing by me, was being bullied and defrauded and pressured into decisions that were not in her best interest, or mine, but clearly only in the best interest of the baby broker and the unnamed adoptive parents.

I wasn't the only one who saw the injustice in this whole situation. My birth mother had some choice words about Mrs. Fielding that the case worker summed up this way:

> *Your birth mother reportedly was quite*
> *upset with this woman [the broker] and*
> *felt that at the very least she had been*
> *taken advantage of. Your birth mother*
> *felt that this woman had also taken*
> *advantage of your adoptive parents as*
> *she was sure that this woman had not*
> *spent all the money they gave her for*
> *hospital and doctor bills.*
>
> *...*

Your adoption by Mr. and Mrs. Chalek was finalized in the Circuit Court of Alachua County on May 5, 1953. The case number is 6815-C.

This is all of the non-identifying information about your birth family that is contained in the closed adoption record. I hope that it is helpful to you in understanding the circumstances of your adoption.

After re-reading the letter several times with a highlighter in hand and a paper close by for taking notes, this is what I had determined.

1. My mother had wanted me, and the separation was painful for her.
2. All of the information I had been using to search was incorrect, at least regarding her last name.
3. I didn't know what her correct last name might be.
4. She was not a pregnant teenager, just a young woman separated from her husband and living on her own.
5. No one knew who my natural (biological) father was, except my birth mother.
   and
6. Mrs. Marquess must have known well the types of worries that plague adoptees.

She had the wisdom to include a description of my birth mother's grief and ongoing concern for me, her relinquished child. I had been wanted. I had been loved.

The unfortunate reality, though, was that I once again faced an apparent dead end. I no longer had any name that I could use to continue my search. I had five wonderful pages of new information. And I was farther from the truth than ever. My hopes were dashed by a single phrase.

Your birth was registered in a purely fictitious name.

Chapter 4

I had nothing but the comfort of Mrs. Marquess' letter to get me through the next three years of fruitless searching. No matter how much the internet opened up the adoption search possibilities, I had nothing on which to base my inquiries. Many of the major players in my adoption were all dead. The doctor, the baby broker, the adoptive parents. Very possibly, my birth parents could also be dead, one or both of them.

If having my questions answered had been the only issue at stake, it might have made sense for me to let my search end with the receipt of that letter. After all, I knew the answers to a few of the most pertinent questions. I knew my birth mother's thoughts and motivations at the time of relinquishment. I knew of her feelings for me. I also understood that reunion might never be possible if she had already passed away.

What still remained, however, was the unanswerable question of my identity and my place in the world. This need to trace one's roots is not limited to adoptees in search of living blood relatives. The popularity of genealogical research is a world-wide phenomenon. Online ancestry forums and paid family tree sites are a booming business, and all because it is part of the natural human condition to seek out and *know* who our ancestors were and what they accomplished, or failed to accomplish. We draw strength from our family lore, and decide whether to emulate our relatives, or to balk family tradition to make our own paths. In this way we are empowered to decide our own fate. We think, "I am just like my father," and it becomes true. Or we think, "I am *nothing* like my father," and also strive to make that a reality, even though we frequently find that our inherited traits and dispositions are harder to escape than we would ever have imagined.

I knew that I had decided I was going to be nothing like my adoptive family. I was glad of it; glad that not a drop of their DNA lived inside my cells. But who was I? Did I have a brother somewhere who looked just like me? Nieces or nephews? A grandfather who would have loved to know me when he was alive, because we had so much in common?

Because of these questions that could never be answered without a chance to ask them in the presence of someone who shared my blood, the letter did not stop me in my quest. It did, for a time, make the search a pointless and dead end task. I talked to a few other "Fielding babies" (as we referred to ourselves) who were conducting searches of their own. None of them had met with any more success than I in obtaining their biological histories. I hired another set of investigators, who took my money gladly and came up empty handed again.

Then, one Monday morning on November 2, 1998, the universe sent me a gift. It came in the form of a newspaper article I read over my morning coffee; an article whose contents caused me to get up out of my chair and hop in my car for a fifteen minute drive to a neighboring town.

The article was a short news piece about a feisty little private investigator named Virginia Snyder, who was under fire for one of her most recent investigations.

Ms Snyder owed part of her fame to her history as one of the first female private investigators to be licensed in the state of Florida. She had made a huge name for herself in the late twentieth century by obtaining evidence sufficient to free several death row inmates, or to get their sentences downgraded. The subsequent fallout was unpleasant for many of the police officers and prosecuting attorneys in the state. She suffered ongoing harassment from the local police force and eventually sued them in return. At his retirement party, one police chief was reported to have hung her picture on a wall where he proceeded to shoot at it, aiming square in the middle of her forehead. It was a dart gun that he held in his hands, of course, but his aim was true. The assembled members of his force were for the most part amused by the performance. They disliked Virginia for their own reasons, mostly because she had denounced them all as incompetent rednecks at one point or another.

The fact that Virginia was, at the time of the party, a 69-year-old "granny" who stood all of 5'2" (and went to great lengths to appear harmless and nondescript) made her quarrel with the police department all the more surreal. But her appearance hid a fierce determination and a passion for justice. That determination, and the nature of the investigation that was profiled in the newspaper article, were what spurred me into action and had me traveling down the road to her little hometown of Delray Beach. Because Virginia had just made national news for locating an adult adoptee's birth mother, and even though the case was turning in a sour direction I held out hope that she might be willing to help me as well.

I entered Virginia's office space in her historic home—the oldest in all of Delray—early on that Monday morning and waited for a chance to speak with her. In my hands I held a copy of the letter from Josette Marquess. While I waited, I conducted a silent argument with myself that centered mainly around not getting my hopes up too high.

When Virginia finally invited me into her office, I found her just as the newspaper described. She was now 77 years old, with short gray hair that framed a round face and friendly eyes. The eyes peered out from behind large rimmed glasses that exaggerated the appearance of age and motherliness. I tried without success to imagine how she had managed to infuriate such a large number of people, all while earning the numerous prestigious awards that lined her walls.

"Mr. Chalek," she said. "What can I do for you today?"

"I saw the article in the newspaper this morning," I said, by way of introduction.

"Ah," Virginia replied. "Yes, I'm afraid we managed to locate someone who clearly did not want to be found."

"That's the thing," I said. I placed my letter on the desk before me. "I would like to find someone, too."

Virginia reached for the letter, pushing her glasses up her nose as she did so.

"Another birth mother search," she said, glancing at the first page.

"Yes. I know it may not be the first thing you want to do right now, with the current publicity and all, but if you read the letter you can see that I think my own birth mother would be quite open to hearing from me."

Virginia looked up at me.

"You know, most birth mothers are, in my experience," she said. "This particular woman in the article is more of an exception than the rule."

I fell quiet, then, and let her return to the letter. When she finished the last page, I blurted out, "There's nothing more I can do, is there?"

She smiled a tight little smile then, and her eyes widened with excitement.

"Oh no, Mike," she said. "I believe there is much you can do."

She laughed, a short barking sound that betrayed a hint of the woman who had taken on whole police forces and won.

"You are holding the smoking gun," she told me. "You've been holding it all along and didn't even know it."

*   *   *   *   *   *

Next, Virginia began to spell out a plan of how I was going to go about walking into the courthouse in Gainesville that very afternoon to present my demands for my adoption record to be opened. Her premise was simple, but powerful.

"The letter says it all right here," she told me. "You even highlighted the sentence yourself. The courts *knew* that your birth mother signed her consent with a fictitious name. They *knew* that the name on your original birth certificate was also false. And most important, pay attention here! The key is, they didn't do anything to fix it. They signed off on the adoption with all of the falsified information."

"Mike," she said. "That's fraud."

"You don't think I need a lawyer to do this?" I asked her.

"Well, if you can afford one, it would help," she answered. "But no, I think you can go right into that courthouse and ask them to show you where they keep the legal forms. Tell the clerk you're filing to have your sealed adoption record opened. She can direct you to where they keep those sorts of requests, the blank templates and such."

"Because of this letter?" I asked.

"It's an official letter, from an official appointee, who looked into the *official* court documents. Yes, I believe it's enough," she said.

I took back the letter and stood up from my chair.

"Thank you," I told her. Despite my increasing nervousness at the audacity of what I was about to do, I felt a strong certainty that she was right and that this would be the most productive step of my entire quest.

"Don't thank me yet," she said. "Thank me when it works."

I left Virginia's house in Delray in a bit of a mental fog. I can't remember much of the four and a half hour drive that I made up to Gainesville. Events were moving at a breakneck pace, and I felt more like I was being carried along for the ride than directing the flow. I also, despite Virginia's assurances and my own sense of certainty, knew that I was a very small individual who was about to take on a very large judicial system.

Well, I thought, *it all worked out for David in the Bible story didn't it? He had five smooth stones and a slingshot to bring down Goliath. I have five sheets of typewritten paper and a fill-in-the-blank legal form.* I pressed down on the accelerator and made my way into Gainesville.

Chapter 5

If you've never traveled to the southern states of the US, your ideas of the deep south probably are based on what you are shown in movies and television. That's all right, because the Alachua County Courthouse in Gainesville is a setting so stereotypically southern that it would have fit right in as the backdrop for any film. It is flanked by huge oak trees whose long tendrils of Spanish moss flow in the breeze. The air is heavy with humidity and the scent of rich earth, even in the winter months. The building itself imparts a sense of tradition and authority to all who pass it by, or enter its hushed and hallowed chambers.

Alachua County has a booming population of, well, a whole 250,000 people. So the courthouse, on that fateful afternoon in November of 1998, wasn't exactly bustling with activity. The clerk eyed me disinterestedly as I approached his desk.

"I'd like to file a petition," I told him.

"Do you have the papers with you?" he asked.

I shook my head.

"I can't give you legal advice or help you fill anything out," he said. "You have to talk to a lawyer for that."

"I know what I want to say. I just need you to show me where to get the blank forms and I'll fill it out myself."

He sighed.

"Ok. Down this hallway you'll find a room that serves as our library. Which form do you need?"

"I want to file to open my sealed adoption records," I said.

The clerk raised his eyebrows at that, but told me how to access a blank form and make a photocopy.

I thanked him and went to retrieve the petition. It took only a few minutes before I was back at his desk.

"I know you said you can't give any advice..." I began.

I could tell that he wasn't going to like me very much. He looked at me wordlessly.

"But I am not sure what I'm supposed to do with this part of the form," I finished.

He waited a few more seconds, obviously deciding how he was going to get rid of me. I kept an innocent and slightly helpless look plastered on my face, hoping for favor.

"It's almost impossible to get those records unsealed," he finally said.

"I know, but I have proof that my adoption was filed fraudulently," I told him.

"Proof?" he repeated.

I opened my file and showed him the letter.

"This letter from the state reunion registry says it,

right here."

The clerk's look was now openly curious.

"Well, then, that's what you say. You are filing a petition to unseal the adoption records, so you've got the name of the document. Now you just write it down. And who committed the fraud? The courts?"

"Sort of, but mostly it was the baby broker and the lawyers and my birth mother, because she signed everything using a fake name and they all knew it."

"Hmm..." he replied. "Well, I can't give you advice. But I've heard that called "fraud on the court" before. That's what I've heard, anyway," he stared at me meaningfully while he related this information.

"Yes," I said. "Yes, that's exactly what I'm saying in here, that they committed fraud on the court."

I was taking furious mental notes, while maintaining a casual and conversational air.

"Well, when you've got it all filled out, you just bring it back over here," he told me.

His meaning was clear. I left his desk quickly and sat down to complete my petition.

When I was finished, this is what I had created: A Motion to Unseal Adoption Records, with a loosely paraphrased reasoning that the birth mother had filed everything with a fictitious name, and that my own birth name was fictitious as well, that the court had known this, and had done nothing to correct it. For good measure, I let the judge know that I had been raised in an abusive and unhappy adoptive home.

I signed the paper, attached a copy of Josette's

letter as a supporting exhibit, and handed the pages over to the clerk.

"Let me call the judge's assistant, the JA," he said.

"Should I leave?" I asked.

"Well, there's no telling when they'll actually consider your petition. But if you want to wait around a bit and come back, there's a good cafe across the street that all the lawyers like to visit on their lunches."

I took his advice and went out for a quick bite to eat. But an abundance of nervous energy drove me back to pacing the courthouse within half an hour.

*　*　*　*　*　*

Surprising both me and the clerk, the JA was soon approaching us across the waiting room.

"Mr. Chalek?" she asked.

"That's me," I replied.

"If you would follow me," she instructed.

We headed upstairs, to the office of one Honorable Robert P. Cates, Circuit Judge of Alachua County Florida.

"The judge has reviewed your petition," the JA told me.

Already? I wondered.

"He would like to know why you want to have your adoption record opened. And he'd like to speak to you personally."

The pace of events was still leaving me breathless. I could only nod in assent.

I was taken into the judge's chambers, where I was seated in front of another large desk, the third time that day I had faced a stranger, ready to tell my story and ask for a miracle.

The judge had a banker's box full of files next to him. A large piece of red tape had been cut off of it.

Judge Cates looked at me as if I were a puzzle he couldn't quite solve.

"I have your petition," he said. "And I have your adoption record."

He gestured toward the box of files.

"I'm curious, Mr. Chalek, what your motivations are in requesting your adoption records be opened."

"Well," I started. I cleared my throat and began again, "I'd like to find my birth mother. I'd like to know who I am. My adoptive parents died years ago, and they were no parents to me at all. I know that my birth mother wanted to keep me. I know she would want to hear from me."

The judge raised his hand to stop me.

"So reunion is your ultimate goal?" he asked.

"Yes," I replied.

"I'm willing to grant your petition," he told me.

I felt the earth move beneath my feet.

And so Goliath falls.

Judge Cates wasn't finished.

"However," he said. "There is protocol to be followed in these circumstances."

More red tape, I thought wryly.

"I must send an order to the Department of

Children and Family Services requiring them to file good reason why I should not release your records to you," he finished.

I thought for a moment.

"Would that be the same department as run by Ms. Marquess?" I asked him.

"It is. And if she can't give me good reason why I shouldn't release your file, I will direct them to produce a copy for you from their microfiched records."

I eyed the original file that I knew was buried somewhere in the box beside him.

"I'll send the letter to Ms. Marquess' office today," he said, ignoring my pointed glance. "We'll be in touch."

I thanked him. The JA showed me out of the chambers.

* * * * * *

Despite the clear victory I had just achieved, I wasn't leaving Gainesville just yet, or the courthouse. I asked the clerk to direct me to the nearest pay phone, and I called Josette's number.

"This is Jo," she answered.

"Jo, this is Mike Chalek," I said. "You wrote me a letter a few years ago, with non-identifying information on my birth mother and my adoption."

"Yes," she said. "I remember."

I didn't ask why she remembered me, one case out of many. I was getting the idea that the fraudulent activity surrounding my adoption was a bit of a big deal, based on the reactions of the clerk, the JA and Judge Cates.

"Well, I filed a petition today in Alachua County to have my adoption records unsealed, because of the fictitious name my birth mother used in the paperwork. And the judge is willing to grant my petition."

"That's wonderful," Jo said. She seemed sincere.

"It's amazing, right? But the thing is, the judge says he is sending you a request for your office to provide good reason why my records shouldn't be opened."

"Has he already sent it?"

"I don't know. But I just wanted to call and see how you might feel about the matter."

"I have absolutely no objections to you getting the contents of your sealed adoption record," she told me. "In fact, you can always see if his office would fax the request over, and I'll get the letter sent back right away."

"Give me your fax number, and I'll go back into the courthouse," I said. I scribbled the number inside my folder.

I'm sure the clerk was thrilled to see my face again.

"Can I talk to the JA one more time?" I asked.

"I'll need to tell her what it's about," the clerk said.

"Well, I've got a fax number to give to her."

The clerk sighed, apparently a common habit of his. He dialed up to the judge's chambers.

In the end, Josette was faxed a copy of the request. And she agreed to fax back a response to the court the next day. By this time, the afternoon was turning to evening. I was still hours away from my home in Boca Raton, so I got in the car and headed back, resigned to waiting for the legal process to grind its way forward.

The days passed agonizingly slowly as I waited for confirmation that the petition was granted. On December 14th I received notice by phone that the judge had signed an order to unseal, and that the copies of my adoption record would be overnighted to me from the Department of Children and Families. Contrary to my perception of an agonizing wait, the entire ordeal ended just a little over a month after I made my unplanned trip to Virginia Snyder's office. I threw my hands in the air in a silent victory celebration and decided there was no way I would be waiting for the truck to show up at my door the next day.

I called Fed Ex and asked them where the shipment was, based on a tracking number I got from Josette. They told me it had left Tallahassee and would be on a plane landing at the main Fed Ex distribution center in Ft Lauderdale in a few hours.

I arrived at the receiving desk for Fed Ex at the Ft Lauderdale airport at six a.m. that morning. I handed over my ID and explained to the attendant what it was that I wanted. I told her I had a package coming in and was hoping that I could grab it before it was loaded onto a truck.

"Um, I think we can do that," she told me. "But that plane hasn't even landed yet, and you'd have to wait."

I waited. About two hours later, she handed over a large cardboard envelope. I signed the receipt and without another word I tore open the package.

The size of the bundled copies was much thicker than I had been led to expect. My understanding was that most adoption records were fairly short and followed a pretty consistent format. Instead, I had what appeared to be a hundred or more pages of blurred, damaged, frequently off-centered documents, many of them transcriptions, that had been copied, microfiched, printed back out and otherwise manhandled. The technology was far from the digitized document storage procedures we have today. I realized that I was never working my way through the packet while standing in the middle of a cold Fed Ex facility in the pre-dawn light.

I put it all back into the envelope and drove to a nearby diner. There I informed the waitress that I would be hanging out for a while, and all I needed was coffee and some privacy. She led me to a booth in the back and obligingly left me alone. I pulled out the papers once more and started reading.

I read once, quickly, through everything that was legible. The most important detail I got from this first reading was my birth mother's real name. Her maiden name was Winnie Faye Higginbotham. She was a Jacksonville local, had been born there in fact. She had been married at the time of my birth to a man named Thomas Yarber, although they each incorrectly believed that the other had filed for and obtained a divorce. So my name on the birth certificate should have been Baby Boy Yarber. In the end, Thomas Yarber had been required to sign his own consent to my adoption once it was discovered that he and Winnie Faye had never legally divorced. Since he was remarried with his own children by that time, it must have been a strange moment indeed: legally signing away another man's child, by a wife he was believed to have divorced. According to the many pages of notes regarding Thomas Yarber, he had led the case workers on a merry chase in their attempts to get his signature. I wondered briefly if he had ever fixed the problem of his divorce and remarriage.

The only other important information I extracted on this first reading were the implied reasons that the courts never obtained a corrected consent from my birth mother. In the beginning of the adoption study, Mrs. Fielding had become embroiled in some legal difficulties regarding a highly publicized lawsuit. She would not give adequate information to the welfare workers on how to locate Winnie Faye, and there was speculation that the lawsuit might have some bearing on her reticence.

I was nine months old by the time the department did locate my birth mother, and between the date of her interview with the case worker and the time of the final hearing, she had once again disappeared. The case worker had also left the agency during the intervening months. No one remained who knew where my birth mother had worked, nor where she might have gone.

Tracking her down would have been too much trouble for them. In the initial contact with Winnie Faye, she had also asked twice if she could possibly get me back. That wasn't the outcome the social workers or the adoptive parents wanted. So they put the file before a judge, falsified information and all, and he added his signature. I frowned at the thought. Such a small-town, small-minded thing for them to do. I reflected again on how much I hated the South. It made me all the more glad that I was planning a move to Colorado at the end of the month.

I had only been in the diner for an hour or so, but I decided that it would take me days to piece together the entire story from all of the various documents and interviews. And making sense of the garbled text wasn't the task I most wanted to pursue in that moment. What I wanted was to take this information back to Virginia Snyder and have her help me find Winnie Faye. Most of the answers I was seeking weren't going to be included in the 108 page adoption record.

I paid my check, jumped in my car, and headed over to Delray Beach.

Chapter 6

Back in Virginia's offices, she and I spent a moment in celebrating our success.

"See, I told you that you could thank me once it worked," she said.

I had become better acquainted with Virginia and her moods and personality in the past few weeks. I knew that she was incredibly pleased with the success of our plan, just as she always took joy in any investigation that resulted in the truth "coming out."

"I want to find Winnie Faye, now," I told her.

"Of course you do," she said.

"Will you help me?"

"No. But Wayne will. Finding people, now that is his greatest calling in life," she replied.

By that, she meant her nephew, Wayne Campbell. He was also a private investigator and did much of the footwork for her; eventually he was slated to inherit the entire business. I knew him to be meticulous and capable, so I gladly turned to him for help.

Instead of taking over the search, Wayne gave me a rundown on how to go about doing it on my own. I left their offices with a game plan, as was becoming the norm. And the best advice he gave me? Start simple. Without giving out too much information, just call around and see who is willing to talk.

I went home, got a copy of the local directories around Callahan, where Winnie Faye had indicated her father was living at the time of my birth. It was close to Jacksonville, and seemed as good a place as any to start looking up the Higginbothams. With a last name like that, I figured I should find someone related to me and Winnie Faye with very little effort.

I made a few calls that first night with no success. But on the following morning I picked up the phone again. I left more messages and sometimes was able to cross a name off of my list until finally I reached a charming old gentleman—he was 90—who claimed to remember my mother very well.

"She was such a cute little girl, blond curls and all," he said. "I don't know where she is now, but I know a woman who was her good friend. Let me give you her number."

I thanked him, and took down the number of a woman who now lived in the town of Stark, Florida.

She answered her phone on the second ring. I felt the stars must be aligning in my favor once again.

"Hello?" she said.

"Hello, ma'am," I replied. "I'm trying to locate my mom, Winnie Faye Higginbotham, and I can't seem to track her down. I was wondering if you might have her number on you."

"Oh, honey," she said. "I don't have her number.

But the last I heard, she and Roy, you know her new husband Roy, they were living in Lanark Village out around Apalachicola Bay somewhere."

"Well that helps. I appreciate it," I told her sincerely. "What was Roy's last name, again?"

"Whitaker, that's his name. And if you reach her, you let her know I send my best, you hear?"

"Yes ma'am," I replied.

I started looking up Whitakers in the Apalachicola Bay area.

Turns out that Lanark Village was a trailer park out in a very rural part of the state. And there was no Roy Whitaker or Winnie Faye Higginbotham listed with that address. Now when I say trailer park, some of my readers may have a very different image in their minds than what I'm talking about. These trailers weren't packed together like sardines in a tin. They were stuck out in dense vegetation, with lots of room between neighbors. There was no HOA or front office I could call and ask for assistance. After another day of wasted inquiries, I did the only logical thing.

I called the police station in their area and told them I needed to reach Winnie Faye because I was related to her and that there had been a death in the family.

They knew her and Roy, and were happy to help.

"Do you have a phone number where you can be reached if we don't find her? Or so she can call you back?"

I gave them my number, and my first name. They

agreed to get on it quickly. So I sat near the phone for the next few hours, waiting and trying to hold my emotions in check. When the phone finally rang, I almost jumped out of my chair.

"Hello," I answered.

"This is Winnie Faye," a strong voice declared. "Who is this that wants to tell me about a death in my family?"

I struggled to find my voice. My stutter was the worst I could remember it ever being. I mastered each word with difficulty.

"Well, actually, there hasn't been a death," I replied. "But I did need to reach you. I was just wondering, does the date January 25, 1952 mean anything to you?"

I thought for a moment that the line had gone dead. Then I heard her voice, much softer.

"Oh my God, yes. You're my son, aren't you?"

She was clearly crying.

"Yes," I told her. "I am."

I remembered that the closed adoption record had mentioned her inability to discuss the relinquishment without crying. She was equally unable to contain her emotions now.

"And they called you Mike? Well, you know, Mike, you've got lots of brothers. One of them lives out in Crawfordville. I just can't do this over the phone. I'm going out to Crawfordville tomorrow to Robert's house, that's your brother. Let me give you his number."

I took down the number and told her I'd call him

immediately to work out some details.

She agreed, and after a call of a few short minutes, she was gone.

It didn't matter. I knew she wanted to meet me, she had even got the ball rolling for us. I worried a little about how Robert might take all of this, whether he knew he had a brother that was given up for adoption. I called him anyway.

When he answered, I explained the situation as quickly and gently as I could. He seemed surprised, to say the least, but didn't have any problems believing the story.

"If I fly up to Tallahassee tomorrow," I said, "Would you pick me up at the airport and take me to meet our mother?"

Our mother. The words left me giddy and elated.

He agreed. I hung up the phone and realized that, once again, my world had changed in a short 24 hours. I had to stop doing this to myself. The emotional strain was enormous.

As exhausted as I felt, I still had a last minute flight to book, and a suitcase to pack.

*   *   *   *   *   *

I used the short flight to Tallahassee as an extra chance to explore the adoption record. I brought along a magnifying glass to help me with the faded and blurry sections. Yes, the copy was really that bad. By the time the flight landed, I had noticed a few other items that were bothering me.

For one, I wondered about the sentence in the opening pages that stated,

Mrs. Fielding is the wife of a Jacksonville police officer who has had a good deal of damaging publicity in the recent suit which an unmarried mother has brought against her, implying black market dealings with babies.

This publicity seemed to have occurred between the time I was born, and the time of the department's first contact with the Chaleks in July, when I was six months old. I made a note to see what I could discover about the lawsuit, once I had more time. Whatever it was, it had been the cause, as later noted in my files, of the Fieldings having to change their phone number and withdraw from the public eye for a while.

Then, I began to piece together how my own adoption had begun as just that, a black market transaction. The Chaleks had heard of Mrs. Fielding and her baby-finding services through someone who worked with Al at the Colgate company, from someone who had also "procured" a baby through her. The Chaleks had paid their $200, brought me home, and might never have begun any legal proceedings at all if it hadn't been for a concerned neighbor who called the Florida Department of Children and Families to report that Adela and Al had an infant in their home, but Adela most certainly had never been pregnant. Why this woman believed that the adoption was anything else than legal and above board is not known. But it was her concern that caused the Chaleks to finally file an official petition for adoption through their lawyer, William D Hopkins. The lawyer's name set off an alarm in my memory. I should know who that is, I thought. I decided to follow up on that as well.

Also, both Al and Adela had reported to the social workers that they were previously married, and divorced. I wondered what the divorce records might reveal about them.

And when the social worker described her first interview with Al, I almost laughed aloud.

Infectious smile, well-spoken, outgoing and likable personality.

Oh yes. That's the salesman we all knew and loved.

Mr. and Mrs. Chalek both participated in the interview...although he took the lead.

And again, I could picture it in my mind's eye. Al would rather have died than let an outsider see him as in any way less than the master of his home, including being master over his wife and her behavior or opinions.

When the social workers had pointed out to my potential adoptive parents that you couldn't just buy a baby and bring him home, that there was a matter of due process to follow, the Chaleks claimed ignorance of the law. They pointed fingers at Mrs. Fielding, her lawyer, the physicians, anyone but themselves. The case workers gave them the briefest of reprimands, then went about the business of trying to ramrod the process through the courts. They obtained consent from the legal father, technically outside of their scope of work. They hand-held the lawyers for both Mrs. Fielding and the Chaleks through each step of the process. They glossed over the details of both Al and Adela's previous marriages (although I wouldn't know that until months later).

In short, they claimed to be in charge of a process that protected infants from inappropriate adoptive placements, all while landing me squarely into a home that viewed adoption as a poor but last-ditch substitute for having a biological child.

I read with alternating sadness and fury of the affection that both Al and Adela had shown for me in that first year of my life. They spoke "proudly" and "warmly" of my good nature, quick development and attractive features. I appeared happy and inquisitive. They were concerned that the birth mother might have legal grounds or the desire to take me back. For a brief moment in time, the Chaleks clearly believed that I was the son they wanted to raise.

It was a far cry from the day when Adela would express the wish that she could send me back into Winnie Faye's womb. But then, it was also years before Adela would give birth to a son of her own womb. To escape this line of thinking, I took a break from my reading. For a while I stared out the plane's window, seeing nothing but a vast expanse of sky above me.

As we approached the Tallahassee airport, all thoughts of my childhood and of the flawed adoption were banished to their dark corners. Instead, I experienced a trepidation and anticipation like nothing I had ever known. Only other adoptees and birth parents who have faced the moment of their own reunions can understand what happens when a primal desire for connection collides head-on with a crushing fear of rejection. I was about to meet my brother, and sleep deprivation and raw emotions had me standing on a razor's edge.

Robert made it easy. We located one another based on our previous descriptions over the phone. He shook my hand and we made our way to his waiting pickup. He explained that the pickup was something he had used in his business as a tile layer. He'd learned the trade from one of Winnie Faye's husbands, a man who had treated Robert like a son, even though he wasn't officially.

That's how the conversation started, and it carried us through until we reached Robert's home. Along the way, I learned that all of my brothers were born with different biological fathers. Robert tried over and over to explain, like a warning, that Winnie Faye was "not like other people," to which I replied that I didn't mind at all. He took it a bit further, saying that the doctors had told them she suffered from bipolar disorder. I shrugged it off. Whatever she was, it was enough that she had loved me at birth and still did.

We pulled into Robert's driveway as the afternoon light was beginning to fade. He had a beautiful place on several acres, and we parked just in front of the open garage.

"Mom's waiting just inside," he said.

"The garage?" I asked.

"Her wheelchair makes it hard for her to maneuver in the house. She wanted some space around her when you showed up to meet," he explained.

It wasn't just Winnie Faye who was waiting for me in the garage. Robert's wife was there as well, and some other family members. But the only person I really remember is my mother. She was older in appearance than I expected, and quite small. Her wheelchair swallowed her up. I walked up and introduced myself, and despite my typically reserved nature, I was soon bending over to give her a hug. After all the introductions were completed, we finally moved into the house.

It was almost Christmas, and everything was decorated for the holidays. Robert's wife Jackie made a big display of being the charming hostess of our impromptu party, but whenever I caught her looking at me, her expression was reserved and cold. I felt instantly unwelcome in her home, but Robert and Winnie Faye made up for the discomfort.

That first night, my mother sat up with me as late as she could bear. She answered a few of my questions, but she had plenty of her own. I tried to be honest about the horrible treatment I'd received from my adoptive family, while trying to keep any hint of blame from falling on her. For her part, she tried to clarify her reasons for relinquishing me, and I told her that I knew a lot of it from the closed adoption record and the transcribed interviews.

One of my mother's particular quirks was her penchant for swearing. Indeed, she could swear like a sailor, and usually did. She told me an incredible history of multiple marriages and lovers, and children born to each one. I began to appreciate my brother's warnings that Winnie Faye was most certainly *not* like other people. She was a ball of fire trapped in a tiny human frame. Her mind jumped from one thing to another, like a hummingbird in the garden, flitting from one flower to the next.

"How long have you been in a wheelchair?" I asked her.

"A while," she replied.

"What is it?"

"Damned if I know," she said. "Doctors, either. They're running more tests all the time. One of these days they'll either figure it out, or it'll just kill me."

After a bit, she excused herself and went to bed. I stayed up at the kitchen table, and soon Jackie retired as well. Robert and I were left alone. For a while the conversation lagged.

"So how did you get the judge to give you your information?" he finally asked me.

Thus began my first attempt to explain the convoluted path that led me to my biological family's doorstep. I took him through the interminable years of searching and dead ends, to the incredible events of the previous two months, and finally ended by telling him of my deep animosity toward the legal system that had ignored a baby selling police captain's wife, clear evidence of fraud, and a department cover up so obscene as to constitute a gross negligence of duty.

Robert gazed at me for a bit. He said, "I know a man you should meet."

"Yeah?" I asked.

"He's a lawyer, a very big name in this state. He's in the Masons with me."

"Ok."

"If you're interested in doing something about the wrongs done to you, he'd be the man to talk to," Robert finished.

"Can you set it up?" I asked.

"Of course," he replied. "I'll call and see what time he can get together tomorrow."

* * * * * *

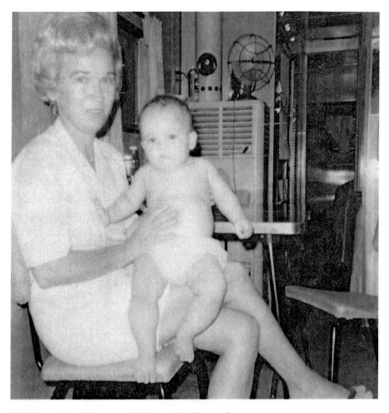

Winnie Faye Higginbotham
Mike's mother
Shown with one of Mike's brothers

I fell asleep late that evening, in a strange bed, just a few steps away from my family who were little more than strangers to me. As tired as I was, I awoke early, with more questions on my mind and a strong desire to see my mother again just to confirm that the whole thing was real. I dressed and made my way to the kitchen.

Jackie and Winnie Faye were already at the table. Coffee was ready and a light breakfast laid out for people to come and go as they pleased. I took a seat next to my mother and asked her how she had slept. She replied that she had slept very poorly, as usual. At this, I saw Jackie grimace briefly.

Talk soon turned back to the topic of the various members of my family. I was having trouble keeping everyone straight.

"Did I tell you that you have a sister?" my mother asked me.

"No," I said, shocked.

"We lost her when she was six," Winnie Faye said.

"How did she die?" I asked.

"Not dead, just gone," she replied. "And it damned near broke my heart, son."

I was more confused now than ever. It must have shown, because Jackie intervened a bit.

"Carol Jean disappeared when she was six," she told me.

"I always thought it was her father that did it," my mother said.

"Her father?"

"Thomas Wagner was his name. He was my second husband. She was born just a year or two after you were," she explained.

"So what happened?" I asked.

"He was from Europe, a handsome devil. The marriage didn't last, of course. There I was busy being a single mother again. I still had Kenneth to care for."

Kenneth, I had discovered, was my older half-brother, the oldest of all the siblings. He was about 18 months when I was born. How my mother had hidden his existence from everyone involved in the adoption was another of my life's strange and inexplicable circumstances.

"So Carol Jean went out to California for a while. To stay with some of her father's relations. We talked on the phone sometimes, and sent postcards, and then one day they told me that she had disappeared," Winnie Faye said.

"There wasn't anything you could do?" I asked.

"Nothing! And I tried. I called every day for the longest time. Then her father moved back to Sweden, and they said the cops out there had dropped the case, that it had gone cold. I've cried my tears over Carol Jean. Plenty of them," she told me.

"Do you have any pictures of her?"

"Of course."

"May I have a copy?"

"I'll get Robert to make you one," Jackie said, interrupting the conversation.

She set a fresh cup of coffee on the table.

"Here mother, I filled it back up for you," she said to Winnie Faye.

Robert came into the kitchen then, grabbing a cup of coffee of his own.

"I got us a lunch meeting with Mallory Horne," he told me.

"The attorney?"

"That's him. If we're going to make it, we should probably shower soon and head on out."

Mallory Horne had an office in Tallahassee, which is where Robert and I headed first. On the way, my brother gave me a little more information on the man we were about to meet.

"You know," he said, "Mallory is quite famous in these parts, and in all of Florida."

"He's that good of a lawyer?" I asked.

"Well, yes, he is. But that's not why he's famous. Not the only reason, anyway. He was on the state legislature for many years. Speaker of the House and President of the Senate both. He saw us through a lot of changes in Florida. And faced down the feds, too."

If Robert had wanted to impress me, it had worked. I was impressed, too, that we could so easily get a last minute appointment with someone like Mallory based on nothing more than my brother's phone call.

"So why is he willing to meet with me?" I asked.

"Because I asked him to do it," Robert replied.

I remembered, then, that my brother had let it slip the night before that he and Mallory were in the

Masons together. I didn't know much about the organization, except that I had heard they were a tightly knit group with a long history which frequently included some of the nation's most influential leaders. If this group membership was at the heart of our hastily scheduled meeting, some of the rumors must be true.

"I could tell you more about him, but he'll just do it himself again anyway when we get there," Robert said.

He grinned.

"Mallory is a character. You'll see."

We parked his truck and entered the respectable old offices that housed Mallory Horne and his partners in law.

And yes, Mallory Horne was quite the character.

He was a tall gentleman, older but not elderly. He spoke like a politician—loud, assured and affable. He had silvery hair and piercing eyes that creased at the edges when he laughed or smiled. But his jokes were anything but grandfatherly. He had a sharp wit, a wicked sense of humor, and an authoritative opinion on everything under the sun.

He offered us a seat in his office, but frequently stood and paced while we visited. He didn't have much time that first day, so after introductions, we got straight to the point.

"Your brother says you have a story he wants me to hear. That you recently represented yourself down in Gainesville and got your adoption records released," Mallory said.

"Yes sir, I did."

"Why? And what more do you think a lawyer could do for you?" he asked.

I had thought about that same question for a long while the night before. I was ready with an answer.

"I want my adoption reversed. And I want our mom, Robert's and mine, to be restored as my legal parent."

Even though I hadn't breathed a word of these thoughts to Robert prior to that revelation, he didn't seem surprised or fazed at all by my request.

Mallory on the other hand, was tempted to laugh me out of his office.

"It'll never happen," he said.

"You don't know the details," I objected.

"Doesn't matter. No one has ever done such a thing before, not to my knowledge. Not even if the parents starved you, killed your dog, made you share a room with the pigs. The courts don't annul adoptions just because the grown adoptee wants to cut his ties."

"Well, they were horrible people, it's true. But that's not the basis of my case," I said.

Mallory stopped pacing for a moment and looked at me curiously.

"All right then," he said. "What is?"

"The whole adoption was based on fraud. Someone down in Gainesville told me it was called 'fraud on the court,' what the social workers and baby broker and doctors all did."

Mallory sat down. He put his hands on his desk and

said, "I guess you better tell me the story. But keep it short if you can."

He listened quietly while I gave him the briefest possible synopsis of how I came to open my court records and what they contained. Sometimes he closed his eyes while I was speaking. Sometimes he gazed at the wall above my head, eyes narrowed in concentration.

When I finished, he still didn't say anything. So I quickly brought up my trusty folder, now stuffed full with both my letter from Josette and the hefty adoption record. I sat it on his desk.

"It's all right there," I said.

"Fraud on the court," Mallory repeated.

"Yes sir."

Mallory looked at Robert. "Did you put him up to this?"

Robert shrugged.

"What do you know about me," Mallory asked me, although he was still looking at my brother.

"That you're well known and well respected. A good lawyer, and once a politician."

"That's it?"

"Yes."

"Before I tell you that I'm considering helping you, I guess you better know a little bit more. I've got my own history that has to do with a fraudulent court case, one that nearly cost me my freedom and my career."

"Oh," I said.

So Mallory proceeded to tell me about the year

when federal investigators tried to destroy him and his highly successful legal practice. It was a powerful story, one in which he ultimately proved the prosecution's case was fraudulent and almost completely fabricated. But the victory cost him dearly. Not even the satisfaction of seeing some of the investigators stripped of their positions and incarcerated was adequate repayment for the damage to his finances, reputation and career.

"I wrote a book about it," he said.

"I'd love to read it," I told him. (He later gave me a signed copy, which I own to this day).

"I'll have my secretary take photocopies of your file here," he said.

"I have originals back at my home, you can keep them."

But he was already on the phone to his secretary.

"Rita," he said. "Can you come in for a moment?"

The secretary showed up a few seconds later. She briskly took the papers to another room, and returned with the copies still warm in her hands. One set she handed to Mallory, the other to me.

Our time was done and Mallory had another appointment. We stood up and shook hands. I thanked him for his interest.

"Leave your contact information with Rita on your way out," Mallory said to me.

"I'll be seeing you later," he told Robert.

Back in the truck, I asked my brother, "Do you think he'll really take it?"

He nodded.

"I do," he said.

We drove back to his home in silence, while I mentally shifted gears and prepared to spend a few last precious hours with my mother.

*   *   *   *   *   *

There were still plenty of questions I had about my family history. I didn't want to pressure Winnie Faye to continue exploring an often painful past, but I knew that her age and health meant that if I went home without getting all of the answers, the chance might feasibly never come again.

She was in a good frame of mind that day, though, and didn't balk at the conversation.

"Your natural father?" she said, unhappily, when I asked about the mystery of my paternal origins.

"Well, his name was John. He was a tall man, came often to the bar where I was working in those days. He liked to drink, was a little rowdy. But he was smart and good looking. He told me he was single, but that was a lie," she added.

"What was his last name?"

"All right, son. All right," she sighed.

"Kirchaine. His name was John Kirchaine. And I was so mad at him I just stopped speaking to him. And that was all. I hid the pregnancy. He never knew a thing about it."

"I read that in the files. Do you think I look like him

a bit?"

She glanced at me, irritated.

"Well I suppose, but I think you look more like me and the Higginbotham side. And that's a good thing," she said.

I hastily assured her that it probably was a good thing. Since she seemed inclined to talk about her own family, I steered the conversation in that direction.

It turned out that the Higginbothams had been in Florida for a long time. A *very* long time.

"Mike, there are characters in our family line that you just wouldn't believe," she said with a laugh.

Stories abounded of famous deeds, of royal charters granted to us in the colonial days, and of rum running pirates and other nefarious individuals, and while she told the stories I made a resolution to look up my family tree back in the genealogical forums to see what I could confirm, now that I had my mother's true identity.

"Your grandfather, he was famous in his own right," she said.

"You mean your father?"

"Yes, my father. His name was Morris, and he ran the biggest moonshine still in Florida, back when I was a girl," she said.

So this is my biological heritage, I thought.

"I'd like any pictures you have, when you are able," I said after the stories were over. "Pictures of you, your parents, anyone really."

"I'll make sure you get some," she agreed.

Eventually, she relaxed a bit, and came out with a story about my birth father.

John Kirchaine, so the legend went, was a formidable man with a wild and unpredictable temper. He had returned from his days as a soldier in WWII with a bit of fire in his bones.

At a bar one night, a few men decided to pick a fight with my father. They harassed him repeatedly while he tried to enjoy a quiet drink.

In the end, John Kirchaine walked out to his vehicle, grabbed a gun, and came back into the bar to blow the heads off of the unsuspecting men.

"But he got off of the charges," Winnie Faye said. "He was friends with someone, a sheriff or judge. Anyhow, he was never found guilty of anything."

I shook my head in awe and more than a little horror.

We stayed up late again that night, as we found more and more things to ask one another.

The next morning, I said goodbye and Robert took me back to the airport.

My leave-taking was low key and remarkably unemotional. We had worn ourselves out and it would be a while before the impact of the last few days would be fully absorbed.

In the truck, Robert and I made light conversation. He asked about my upcoming move to Colorado. I thanked him for everything he had done to arrange my reunion with the family, and for introducing me to Mallory. We parted ways congenially at the airport curb.

Carol Jean
Mike's half-sister
Missing since the age of 6

John Kirchaine
Mike's biological father
Picture courtesy of Kirchaine family

John Kirchaine
Mike's biological father

Morris Higginbotham
Winnie Faye's father
and Mike's grandfather

Chapter 7

Christmas of 1998 hardly registered on my calendar at all. I had met my family in the weeks prior, and the unexpected trips around the state had left me short on time to pull off the planned cross-country move. So Christmas Day found me busy dealing with moving trucks, boxes and the various complicated logistics of leaving one place of residence in order to occupy another. I hadn't spent an actual Christmas holiday surrounded by parents or siblings in my entire adulthood, so I didn't suffer any overwhelming sadness that another solitary day was upon me. I wondered briefly how my family might be celebrating. Then I went back to dealing with the moving boxes.

I didn't give Mallory Horne much time to get through the holidays before I was calling him to follow up on our possible court case. The longer I had to think about it, the more appeal I found in the idea that I could take all of the fraudulent, destructive and negligent behavior of the Florida adoption system and use it as a basis to ask them to give me back my birth identity, at least in name. That much I believed the system owed to me and Winnie Faye both.

So I admit it; I pestered Mallory. I wanted to know what I could do to help make sure I had the strongest possible case, while he decided if he wanted to help me pursue it.

"Document everything," he said.

"More than what's in the record?" I asked.

"There's plenty that's not in that record, Mike. The caseworkers discussed the Chalek's previous divorces, but those records aren't copied in the file. And they make reference to your mother's missing divorce from Thomas Yarber, but what if it actually happened and the state just missed it? If Thomas Yarber signed off on your consent and he wasn't actually the legal father, it would make just one more nail in the coffin," he said. "You can never have too strong of a case, Mike. Never."

"I had another thought too," I told him. "I'm worried that maybe I should have disputed that will after all. Does it make me look like I was admitting to some kind of guilt, that there really was some 'good reason' that I deserved to be left out and disowned that way?"

"I don't think you need to worry about that," he said.

"When you take the case, I am going to want to find out what Al meant, you know. Even if we have to subpoena Glenn into the courtroom to do it," I replied.

"I'll be in touch at some point soon to let you know my decision," he said.

We hung up the phone with the understanding that I would check in on him personally when I made my next trip out to Tallahassee, which was scheduled for later in January. I would be staying with Robert for several days while I attended to a few matters, including keeping myself firmly in the forefront of Mallory Horne's thoughts.

While I waited, I put my hard earned researching skills to the test. I started finding out what I needed to do to request copies of the Chalek divorces, and how I could look through the old files for any mention of a document concerning individuals with the last names Chalek, Sutton, Higginbotham or Yarber, even if I only knew approximate dates to search. I planned a circuit of the various county repositories so that I could maximize my time in Florida.

Then I got on a plane and left my beautiful new home in the Rocky Mountains. I wasn't thrilled about returning to my "birth" state, but I also felt a compelling need to see my case through to the end. And I wasn't going to turn down the chance to spend a little more time with my family. So Robert picked me up at the airport once again and I got busy working on a case that didn't even technically exist—yet.

My court record searches were a mixed bag of results. I had great success with Alex and Adela, identifying the dates and case numbers of both of their previous divorces. To my shock (although nothing should have surprised me at that point), I found that Adela had lied to the caseworker and the courts. She had actually been married and divorced *twice* before her marriage to Alex, as opposed to once as she had sworn in the adoption petition. I went ahead and ordered and paid for copies to be sent to my home documenting all seven events: four marriages and three divorces.

Back in Gainesville, I went to find the original chancery book where my adoption petition, a public document, had first been located back when Doug Diamond and I were working on it. The record, the entire book in fact, was nowhere to be found.

I left the archives and went upstairs, asking the clerk where I might track down the missing ledger.

"That book is no longer available to the public," he told me.

"Do tell," I replied.

"It was a staff decision," he said, betraying just a hint of defensiveness.

"I'd like to talk to whoever is in charge of giving the thumbs up on that type of decision," I told him.

He directed me across the street to the courthouse, telling me I should ask for Karen.

I went straight over, and soon had the manager of official records standing before me.

"I'm looking for the chancery book that has the filing of my adoption petition," I told her.

"What years would that be?" she asked.

I told her. It was a ridiculous question, she knew exactly which book was missing.

"That book has been removed from circulation," she said.

"It's a public record," I replied. "You don't have

that right or authority."

"It was a staff decision. That book is simply not fit for public consumption, so it has been moved to a new location."

"I'd like to talk to your superior," I said.

"That's not going to happen."

"Then I would like a copy of the page that relates to my own adoption petition."

"I would be glad to do that for you, as long as you realize that it will be redacted to remove any identifying names."

"You would white out a public document?"

"It is the decision of this staff that we will do so, yes. In the public interest."

The conversation had become so inane, and so circular, that I gave up. I thought once again, *only in the redneck, backwards, backwater, small town, small-minded deep South...*

You get the picture. I may have said it before, that I'm a little prejudiced when it comes to a certain part of the country. I tell myself that I'm moderately justified in holding these opinions, even if they're not true.

I called Mallory and let him know what had happened.

"Don't you have those copies somewhere in your files?"

"Well maybe, but I just moved, Mallory. I haven't even pulled everything out of boxes yet."

"Mike," he sighed. "I know I told you to document everything. But I'm pretty sure that if a judge needs to see what's in that chancery book, he can override the staff decision and have it on his desk in a matter of minutes."

"Got it," I replied.

"I understand your frustration," he said.

"I'll let you know what else I find."

*　*　*　*　*　*

These are the primary characters involved in my story of a black market purchase that became a hastily finalized adoption:

Alex D. Chalek—Adoptive Father

Al had been married and divorced once before, as he had indicated to the court. The caseworkers verified this by sending a short "confirmation request form" to the county of the marriage and divorce proceedings.

The welfare department, as they were known back then, did not request a full copy of the divorce, either the petition or the decree. If they had requested these documents they would have discovered that Al's first wife sued him for divorce on the grounds of *extreme and repeated cruelty*.

It was not an unsupported claim. In the complaint, his wife documented three specific dates when Al had struck her: twice in the face and once with a shove that threw her violently across the room. Not only did his soon-to-be ex-wife swear to these charges in court, she brought along a corroborating witness.

Although Al denied all allegations, the judge granted his wife her divorce and also her request that Al be required to pay all associated court and attorney fees. The year of the divorce was 1944. At the time, Al was still an active member of the US Air Force, as noted in the decree. Just two weeks after his divorce was granted, Al married Adela. Both of them lied on the application and said it was their first marriage each.

I also discovered more about Al's service in the armed forces. The closed adoption record said that he had enlisted several times, and had been variously a fighter pilot or a member of the Navy's counter-intelligence unit. Since the work in counter intelligence was something Adela had mentioned to the caseworker in passing, I had briefly wondered if it might not be a bit of exaggeration or bravado that Al had used to impress her when they were dating.

Once I obtained a copy of Al's military service and discharge papers I was able to confirm that Al had, in fact, been both a fighter pilot and a part of military counter intelligence, although with the Army and not the Navy. According to his Summary of Military Occupations, he had conducted investigations of sabotage, sedition, espionage, and civilian personnel or property [which] were involved.

When I thought about it, the profile of such a soldier, someone who had served in those types of positions as a part of the second world war and its aftermath, supported his development into the overbearing, manipulative, pathologically disciplined man that I had known as my adoptive father. And his skills and training would also explain how he could take off one face and put on another outside of our home, the face of a charming, handsome salesman who was at ease with the world and himself.

To say the least, Al had a few skeletons in his closet, some warning signs that the welfare department had clearly missed. But these were nothing compared to what Adela had been hiding. Her past was a clearly documented path through a troubled and dysfunctional adolescence into a violent and equally troubled adulthood.

Jessie Eula Adela Sutton Chalek—Adoptive Mother

At first glance, the marriage applications for Adela were fairly standard. Three applications, three marriages, all in the state of Florida and with only the name of the husbands changing from one form to another.

However, as I looked at each of the marriage licenses and applications and compared them closely, I noticed an odd discrepancy. Her age at the time of marriage to Alex was inconsistent to the ages and dates of the other two marriages.

On the first marriage application, Adela's mother had been required to sign a consent because Adela was underage. On the application it stated that Adela was sixteen, and her mother consented to the union.

This marriage took place to a man named Perry, who was 23, seven years older than Adela. They were married in October of 1940.

The second marriage was to a man named Joseph. The application was dated in March of 1943, and Adela listed her age on that application as being 20 years old. No matter what form of math I employed, I couldn't create a scenario in which Adela had celebrated four birthdays in a span of less than three years. I chalked the whole thing up to human error and proceeded to examine the third application for marriage, the one in which she and Alex were joined in holy matrimony in January of 1945. At this point, Adela listed her age as 21 and that should have cleared up the matter and been the end of it.

However, something still struck me as odd about the ages and dates. I knew that the closed adoption record had information on Adela's age and birth date at the time of my adoption hearing. I pulled out the appropriate pages for comparison.

In the adoption petition, Alex Chalek is described as being 31 and Adela as 25. The year was 1953. I grabbed my pen and paper and went back to computing years, ages, and possibilities.

From the date of the Chaleks marriage in 1945 to the date of my adoption hearing in 1953, over eight years had passed. Which meant that Adela's age should have been 29 or 30. Now I understand that for many people 30 is a significant milestone and one they may dread admitting, but lying to the court as a matter of pride seemed an extreme measure—even for my adoptive mother, the master of extreme measures.

I wondered, had she lied about her age to Al when they were dating? Did she feel compelled to maintain the lie? Or were one or more of the previous marriages the real instance of a fabricated age?

Enough of this, I thought.

It was time to find a more authoritative source of Adela's birth date and proper age.

Fortunately, there were two. Adela's death records and the detailed welfare department recommendation in the adoption file. Both of these referred specifically to Adela's date of birth as December 15, 1926.

So, working backwards, Adela had just turned 18 when she married Al.

She was 16 when she married Joseph.

And she was a mere 13 years old when she married her first husband, Perry, a man *ten years* her senior.

Dear God, I thought.

Not only had Adela lied on the marriage application, so had her mother.

What in heaven's name could convince a mother to do such a thing?

The answer to that question was long gone to the grave, along with Adela, her mother and the first husband.

What remained, however, were the divorce petitions. Still slightly sick to my stomach from the disturbing revelations, I opened the divorce files for Adela and started reading.

(If anyone still has questions regarding the validity of Adela's birth date, the recently opened federal census from 1940 confirms that she was born in 1926).

When she was 14, Adela filed for divorce from her first husband, citing not only a "violent and ungovernable temper" (a common legal term in those days), but also "excessive cruelty." For an entire year she had been trapped in a child-marriage to a man very much her senior, and her allegation was that he treated her cruelly and abusively.

What effect might this diseased relationship have had on a young girl's emotional development? I only had to look at the second divorce to find my answer.

The second husband filed for divorce after a short six weeks of marriage. In court, he testified to a repeated sequence of promiscuity and fits of rage on Adela's part. Quoting directly from the divorce petition:

> *Plaintiff further represents that during the time that he and the defendant lived together as man and wife that she frequently and without any justification or excuse flew into fits of anger, cursing and abusing your plaintiff.*

> *Plaintiff further represents that the defendant immediately after his marriage to her began associating with other men, going out at night with them and*

spending a great portion of her time sneaking out with men, notwithstanding, the fact that your plaintiff was endeavoring to keep her from doing so.

Plaintiff further represents that each time he accused her of going out she would fly into a fit of temper, cursing and abusing your plaintiff, but she would continue to go out each day and night and when your plaintiff would try to make her stay at home she would fly into fits of anger, cursing and abusing him. Which fits of ungovernable temper she exhibited daily until finally six weeks after his marriage to her she deserted your plaintiff...

The husband's father also testified at the hearing, because the young newlyweds were living in his parents' home during their brief marriage.

Q: How did they [the newlyweds] get along?

A: Right after they were married his wife started to walking off from the house and coming up town and meeting soldiers and going to Lake Bradford and Wakulla Springs and around and when she would come home Joe my son would get after her about where she had been and she would fly into a fit of temper cursing him and carrying on like a crazy person. She would tell him that she had not done any thing wrong just rode around with the soldiers. We tried to talk to her but she would not pay any attention to any of us...

Q: Did you ever see her with soldiers?

A: Yes sir, I have seen her with them and they have come by the house to get her. My son had to go [to work] and then the soldiers would come by the house at night and get her...

Q: How often would she get mad?

A: It was every day, from the time they were married.

For her part, Adela responded the the petition in the following manner:

Comes now the Defendant...as for answer says; That she neither admits nor denies the allegations contained in said

Bill of Complaint and that she rests within the sound discretion of the Court the granting or denying of divorce as prayed for...further, that she waives any further or other notices of subsequent hearings that may be had in said cause.

I was jealous, briefly, of her ex-husband's ability as an adult to end his abuse at Adela's hands. I had no such recourse as a child when she flew at me in a rage. The law provided protection to him, while Adela proceeded to find a new outlet for her ever simmering anger.

The mention of Wakulla Springs as a place that the soldiers would frequently take Adela brought up a long-buried memory. Boots would frequently reminisce when I was little about the time that she had been cast as an extra in a famous black and white Tarzan movie that was filmed in Wakulla Springs. I guessed that her pronounced beauty, especially in her younger years, was one of her few sources of pride. Family members confirmed that it was true, Boots had once acted in the classic film as a stand-in for Jane Goodall, Tarzan's love interest.

Too bad for me that she hadn't pursued a career in acting and taken herself to Hollywood.

Lenora Fielding—Baby Broker

I cast my net far and wide as I sought to document every lie, every fabrication and every crime of omission that had been woven into my fraudulently finalized adoption. But even then, I only completed my investigation with help from some of the most unexpected places. I owe a debt of gratitude, in particular, to a kind stranger I met on a flight to Atlanta.

I had been puzzling for a while over the question of the supposed lawsuit and "recent publicity" that had caused such discomfort to Lenora Fielding around the time of the adoption study. I wanted to know what the charges had been, and whether the birth mother had won her claim. The way the adoption record had phrased it in transcribing the first home study visit with Adela, was this:

> *Mrs. Chalek was a little reluctant to discuss the means by which they secured this adoptive baby, but finally brought out that they got him through Mrs. Fielding in Jacksonville. Mrs. Fielding is the wife of a Jacksonville police officer who has had a good deal of damaging publicity in the recent suit which an unmarried mother has brought against her, implying black market dealings with babies...while they were waiting to hear further from Mrs. Fielding, the publicity came out about the other case, and the Chaleks were very much concerned. It was at this point they got in touch with Attorney William D Hopkins, since Mrs. Chalek comes from Tallahassee and had*

> *known Mr. Hopkins personally, in*
> *addition to having him secure her*
> *previous divorce for her. <u>Mr. Hopkins is</u>*
> *<u>also State's Attorney</u>.*

I underline this last bit, because I realized after my fourth or fifth reading of the closed adoption file the reason why the name William Hopkins sounded so familiar to me. This "family friend" of Adela's, who helped finalize my fraudulent adoption in concert with a notorious black market baby broker, was none other than the State Attorney of Florida from 1947-1973. Bill Hopkins, as he was otherwise known, had created a huge name for himself in 1959—just six years after my finalized adoption—when he convinced an all-white jury to find a group of young white men guilty of assaulting and raping a black female student from Florida A&M. In the case, he argued persuasively that the *consistent* enforcement of law is a necessary function of the system.

Bill Hopkins would also, as the Chalek family attorney, be the man who handled defending Glenn when he and a girlfriend got in trouble for armed robbery as a young man, long after I had left the family. Family lore said that Hopkins had made the entire thing disappear, sealed up as if Glenn had been a minor at the time (which he was not).

I wondered which of Adela's divorces had been secured by Mr. Hopkins. I supposed it must have been the first, when she was 14, not that it mattered much, except for the likelihood that if he were a close friend of the family and their regular legal counsel, he would have had to have known about Adela's repeated fraudulent reporting of her age. I pushed the matter out of my mind to focus on the problem of Mrs. Fielding and her black market baby ring.

I had thoughts of the Fieldings and the mystery lawsuit firmly in mind as I boarded a plane bound for Georgia in the spring of 1999. I took my seat and opened a notebook to begin sketching out more to-do lists and plans for how to find more old records to strengthen my case against the state of Florida. I remained absorbed in my task throughout take-off and well into the flight.

Eventually, I closed the notebook and glanced at the passenger seated next to me. She was a middle aged businesswoman, who had a book in her hands and a bag of complimentary airline peanuts on the tray in front of her. She must have caught a bit of motion as I turned, because she glanced up from her book and smiled. Pretty soon we had introduced ourselves and were making small talk.

I have never been shy about sharing my life story or talking about adoption issues with random strangers. I know that it is only through our stories that adoptees can help gain the broad understanding necessary to change the closed adoption laws. So I gave my fellow passenger a brief rundown of what I was working on, and why.

She seemed very interested, and sympathetic.

"How strange," she said. "I'm from the Jacksonville area, you know."

"You live in Duval county?" I asked, probably a little too excitedly.

"I sure do," she said, smiling.

"That's perfect!" I said.

"Why's that?"

"Because I need someone who lives down there to help me either get a copy of this mysterious lawsuit or who can help me find a trustworthy individual to go on my behalf," I said.

"You know," she replied, "your story is just fascinating enough that I'll do it myself."

"I can't tell you how much I would appreciate it," I said. "Let me give you my mailing address in case you find anything."

There was no real reason to believe this person would follow through on our hasty agreement, but a few weeks later I received a letter in the mail. Inside was a true and certified copy of a lawsuit filed against Lenora Fielding in 1952 by a claimant named Rebecca Cobb, Case #20657-L, Duval County, Florida.

Ms Cobb alleged the following in her complaint:

> *On or about June 18, 1952 the defendant [Mrs. Fielding] did falsely imprison the plaintiff and held plaintiff without just or probable cause in defendant's house, and by physical force tried to restrain her from moving to another place of abode. Further, the*

defendant refused upon plaintiff's request to relinquish plaintiff's clothing and other personal belongings, which defendant retained by reason of a debt which defendant falsely alleged to be due to her from plaintiff.

Plaintiff ... further charges the defendant, on, to wit, June 18, 1952, did assault and batter the plaintiff, laid hands on the plaintiff and shook her, and attempted to drag plaintiff into defendant's home, and used toward plaintiff language of a rude and insolent nature, threatening plaintiff and calling her vile names; whereupon plaintiff broke away from defendant and fled down the street in tears and humiliation and in bodily fear of the defendant.

Plaintiff...further alleges that on or about June 18, 1952 the defendant did slander the plaintiff in that she did say to another, with intent to humiliate and degrade plaintiff, and with malice, that plaintiff was an unwed mother, and a slut, and a person not fit to associate with, and that plaintiff was a thief.

Further, on or about June 20, 1952 the defendant did say to another, with the intent to humiliate and degrade the plaintiff, and with malice, that plaintiff was a slut and a whore and was sleeping with every married man in the neighborhood...

Plaintiff says that all of the utterances of the defendant as alleged herein were and are false, and were uttered maliciously and with the intent to expose plaintiff to scorn and contempt.

I knew enough about the adoption industry of the mid-20th century to read between the lines and to know that what Ms Cobb described in her lawsuit was an accurate picture of many of the "maternity homes" that came to define the Baby Scoop Era.

Maternity homes were little more than boarding houses where families sent their unwed pregnant daughters during the "visible" portions of their pregnancies. The social stigma associated with children born out of wedlock and the double standards regarding male and female sexuality meant that many young pregnant women, who had received little-to-no sexual education and had zero access to birth control, were treated worse than common criminals. They were sentenced to a type of incarceration in the maternity homes, and were often told, "You can come home, but not if you bring back a baby."

For older single mothers who didn't have the same family pressure to relinquish their babies for adoption (women like Ms Cobb), the maternity homes developed another fail-safe strategy. If a mother decided, after living in the home during any portion of her pregnancy, that she did not want to relinquish her child, she would be presented with an astronomical bill for room and board and often be subjected to verbal and psychological abuse much like what was described by Rebecca Cobb in her allegations.

There was no longer any question in my mind that what Mrs. Fielding was running out of her Jacksonville residence was a maternity home, and one of the more destructive ones. I knew from the caseworker's notes in my adoption file, and also from conversation with Winnie Faye, that Mrs. Fielding had applied enormous pressure to the birth mothers to get them to put a falsified name on the hospital records and birth certificates. Family rumors over the years, and my adoptive parents' many hateful insinuations, indicated that the $200 the Chaleks testified that they paid to Mrs. Fielding for the birth mother's expenses was far under what they actually paid to the baby broker to secure my transfer.

Later, I also found copies of newspaper clippings regarding the Cobb vs Fielding lawsuit. One of them gave a little more insight into the State Welfare Board's attitude toward the Fielding operation. A representative called Ms. Cobb's allegations a beginning for stopping the state-wide baby selling racket they were fighting on multiple fronts. The representative also indicated that the welfare board had been investigating Ms Fielding for many years prior to this incident. Also, according to

Ms. Cobb's testimony, four other girls had given birth during the time that she lived in the Fielding home. Each of the birth mothers was paying room & board, while the adoptive parents handed over an unknown sum of their own to "acquire" the infants.

Unfortunately, the lawsuit was dismissed in 1954 because Ms. Cobb had left Jacksonville before the matter could be heard. It seems that Lenora Fielding's baby selling days were over, however. After 1952 I could find no more mention of her in conjunction with private adoptions, and I haven't met or talked with any other Fielding babies whose birth dates would contradict this assumption.

* * * * * *

What I saw before me now was a clear legal argument for having my adoption annulled and my birth certificate reinstated with my mother and legal father as the parents. I also wanted all of the Chalek's parental rights rescinded (posthumously of course), and I was hoping to convince Mallory to sue the lawyer, William Hopkins, as well.

I sent Mallory copies of everything I had discovered, and I summarized the case as I understood it:

> *My birth mother contacted Mrs. Fielding because she was afraid that she would be unable to adequately care for me and*

thought an adoption would be in my best interests. She had no problems with registering my birth in her real name, but came under extreme pressure from a known black market baby broker to use a false name. When the state welfare worker initially phoned her, she asked if she could have me back. When they met in person, she asked again if she could have me back. The worker persuaded her that if she cared about me, she would leave me with my adoptive parents, and that the state would put significant barriers to my return if she pursued that line of inquiry.

In the meantime, my adoptive parents had been reported to the welfare board and it was discovered that they had not obtained a legal adoption of me, they had simply brought me home from the hospital and called it good. They indicated to the social workers that they had avoided the approved adoption agencies because of the extensive wait times and the likelihood that their application would be rejected. No one questioned what that meant. But they also lied about and covered up their marital histories and problems with violence and instability.

The lawyer for my adoptive parents was also the State's Attorney, and it is likely that his elevated position may have unduly influenced the court to look the other way when it came to the known falsified information on my birth mother's consent and on my birth certificate.

The baby broker was also well connected, and was being pursued by the welfare board for her black market activities.

I can't see why, after taking all of these facts into account, a judge would not feel compelled to grant me my requests.

After I provided Mallory with the proof and with my list of requests, I felt certain that he would agree immediately to take the case.

Instead, on April 20, 1999, Mallory Horne sent me a letter declining to take my case. He blamed it on the distance between his office in Tallahassee and the courts in Gainesville where the motions would be filed and heard. He additionally stated that he was concerned that I was so "emotionally charged" that winning the legal battle would not bring me any closure.

I held his letter in my hands and for the briefest of moments, gave in to the overwhelming surge of disappointment.

Chapter 8

In the end, I wasn't any better at taking "No" for an answer than I had ever been in my adult life. So I picked up the phone and called my brother, Robert. He had started this ball rolling, he was going to help me keep it that way.

"Robert, you've got to call and talk to Mallory," I said when my brother answered the phone.

"What's this all about?" he asked.

"He says he's not going to take my case. You need to call and convince him to change his mind. Use the 'bonds of brotherhood' argument, or whatever it is that the Masons call it. But get him to take the case," I pleaded.

"All right, Mike, I'll call him. Don't worry about it, he'll come through," Robert told me. His calm was unshakable.

I thanked my brother and hung up.

It worked, playing the trump card the way that I had. Two days later, Mallory changed his mind. Instead of sending me a letter, though, this time he called me to let me know of his decision.

"I guess I'm taking your case after all," he said,

dryly.

"It's a good case, Mallory," I told him.

"No one has ever won anything like this. If I lose, it will really give me a black eye around here."

"We're not going to lose," I said. "I can feel it, like when I filed that petition to open the records. We're going to win this thing."

"You're crazy, Mike, you know that. But maybe you're right. If the evidence wasn't there, no amount of arm twisting would get me to take this into court."

I figured that it was as good a time as any to ask him to take on another giant. I wanted to sue the daylights out of the State's Attorney who had ignored all of the signs that I was a black market baby and had helped to cover up his clients' attempt to circumvent the system.

So I asked. And Mallory's response was absolute.

"I am not suing Bill Hopkins," he said. "I know him, he's a friend. And there wouldn't be any point."

Not wanting to test our new partnership any further, I reluctantly decided to let the matter of William Hopkins fall by the wayside.

Over the next several months, Mallory filed all of the motions necessary to combine my pro-se petition to open with our new Petition for Annulment of Adoption and Termination of Parental Rights and For Amendment of Certificate of Live Birth. Yes, it was a mouthful. I was asking for a complete and total break with my adoptive family, as if it had never happened at all.

Winnie Faye was in enthusiastic support of the

efforts. As a matter of fact, once the media became aware of the upcoming trial they were interviewing anyone and everyone they could reach. My mother still didn't have a phone, but one intrepid reporter was able to track her down. She supported my case both in that brief interview and in deposition with Mallory. Her desire to have our familial bonds reinstated was one of the central arguments of our petition.

In the meantime, it was discovered that Winnie Faye was suffering from advanced multiple sclerosis. It was the reason she was confined to the wheelchair, and it took a toll on both her physical and emotional well being. Our conversations became more erratic than ever, sometimes deteriorating into tirades. She became angry with Robert and had a complete falling out with him and Jackie. I was glad to have her support and to have found my mother when I did, but it was painful to watch her slow descent into a horrible disease.

From the time we filed our motions in June of 1999 to our day in court in mid December, life was a flurry of activity. I was trying to direct my involvement from thousands of miles away, and eventually I gave it up and arranged an extended stay with Robert and Jackie throughout November and December. The atmosphere in their home on this trip was remarkably uncomfortable. Jackie barely disguised her distaste for me, and I spent more time with Mallory than with my brother, partly to avoid the pointed stares of my sister-in-law.

Mallory and I became great friends during this

time, a friendship that would endure until his death many years later. He forgave me for the somewhat dastardly trick I had played in using my brother to get to him. I came to admire him greatly, and he became more of an uncle to me than any of my adoptive or biological relations ever would be. He frequently told me, with gusto, that when it was all over I was to write a book and he'd back up "any damned thing I wanted to put in there." Then he'd point to the box of cigars on his shelf and tell me to be ready, because we were both having a good smoke when we won this thing.

As my lawyer, Mallory came to know my story backwards and forwards, although it frequently happened that I would surprise him with a previously forgotten detail. When I read through Adela's records from her second divorce and remembered her stories of acting in the Tarzan movie, I naturally told Mallory. He replied by telling me that he, too, had been one of the local youths who took a part as one of the extras on the film. He clearly remembered the pretty girl who had stood in for Jane, and we marveled at the strange coincidence that he had once been acquainted with Boots in her youth.

Getting back to work, we agreed to try and track down my elusive adoptive brother in time for any hearings. We attempted service on Glenn multiple times, requesting his presence to answer questions and testify as to the remarks in Al's will and to defend the virtual hostage he had taken of my personal items and records. Glenn managed to avoid service every single time. No one has found or talked to him to this day.

Mallory was certain we wouldn't need the testimony. But I was denied my final hope of getting back my grades, photos, and scouting awards, including the Eagle Badge. I began to wonder if they hadn't all been destroyed, and the thought was a painful one.

In the meantime, another of the strange coincidences that marked my story happened as I came to know Mallory's secretary, Rita, through Mallory's suggestion. Rita performed many investigative services in her role as secretary. She invoiced me for her time as often as Mallory did. One day, when Mallory had to leave unexpectedly for a last minute deposition, he suggested that I invite Rita to lunch instead since he had to cancel on me.

So I did, I walked out to her desk and said,

"Mallory thought you might like to go to lunch with me."

She rolled her eyes. "Oh he did, did he?"

"It's all right if you don't. Doesn't make a difference to me," I replied.

But she was already gathering up her things.

"No," she said. "I've always been curious about some of the details of your life that aren't in all this paperwork. Let's go get something to eat, and maybe you can fill me in."

And so began another friendship. Rita, it turned out, was an adoptee herself. Her adoptive father had for many years been mayor of a little town called Sopchoppy, and he even had a park there named after him. We chatted about her family, and about my personal history, until finally she mentioned that she had grown up in a house that was once the main roller skating rink for the entire county.

Her remarks stopped me dead in my tracks. I looked at her across the table, my fork halfway to my mouth.

"You're kidding," I said.

"No, really. It was wild," she said. "This big huge room in the middle of our house, with a scuffed up wood floor and the names of every kid who ever skated there carved into the beams that hold up the walls."

"I know about that place," I told her.

"How?"

"Boots used to talk about it *all the time*. About how she would go out there with friends and the fun they would have."

Rita shook her head.

"It's a small world..." she sang.

I laughed.

"Seriously, could you take me to see the place sometime?"

She thought about it.

"I don't see why not. I guess we could run out this weekend if you've got the time."

I had the time. We planned a trip for the coming Saturday.

The car ride to Sopchoppy was a pleasant one. Rita was good company, and as we traveled she filled me in on little bits of local lore. She told me more about her father, and for once I didn't feel the need to talk about my own life, or the details of the case, or of anything in particular. The miles passed quickly and we soon pulled up to the old southern house that was Rita's childhood home.

They were in the process of renovating the living/dining room that used to be the roller rink. It was vast and empty of furniture, and we walked around the perimeter of the room, reading out names and dates and strange sayings that children had carved into the walls. I was the one who found it first, the name "Boots" clearly carved in an awkward hand, along with the names of some of her sisters. I called Rita over, and together we shook our heads.

How odd, I thought. *How very, very odd.*

I imagined that the name must have been carved there about the time that she was first getting married. A thirteen-year-old child, carving her name into the roller rink wall, about to marry a man who would violently abuse her and change her life forever. I didn't forgive her in that moment, but for a second, I pitied her.

Rita and I returned quietly to Tallahassee. I thanked her for taking me, and we agreed that it was about time to bring my whole sordid past to a close. The court date was only a few days away.

* * * * * *

On December 13, 1999 the county courthouse was

abuzz with a room full of reporters and photographers. Judge Maurice V Giunta took one look at the assembled crowd and announced,

"I will NOT have the dignity of this court compromised any further by turning this into a media circus. We will move this hearing to my chambers, now."

I objected immediately, earning a stern look from my lawyer.

"I think that such a move is in violation of my civic rights, your honor," I said. "I would like to have the press witness these proceedings."

The judge ignored the impropriety of my address, and said, "One member of the press may accompany us. Who will it be?"

A reporter named Ron Word, whom I had come to know rather well over the past few months, stood up and said that he would be glad to represent the interests of the press.

Together, Mallory Horne, Ron Word, the attorney for the state, and Josette Marquess (my only witness) accompanied me to the judge's chambers.

There, we gathered around a large rectangular table. The judge seated himself at the head.

"Mallory," he said, "Let's get this over with."

"Thank you Maurice," Mallory replied.

Maurice? I thought. *Great, they're friends. He knows everyone, doesn't he? From Tallahassee to Gainesville and everywhere in between.*

Despite the small gathering, Mallory stood up and

made an opening statement worthy of any televised courtroom drama. He spelled out the events of my life in moving detail, and gave a thorough explanation of the legal basis of our petition.

When he was done, even I was slightly speechless at the power this man could wield over a court.

"And now," he said, "I think my client would like to say a few things on his behalf."

He gestured to me.

But before I could open my mouth, Judge Giunta interrupted.

"I'm sure he has plenty of things to say," he said. "But the court has no need to hear them."

I gaped in shock, but before I could make a scene, the judge turned to Josette.

"Mrs. Marquess, what is your department's position on the matter of this petition?" he asked.

Josette answered briefly that she and her department were in support of my request to annul the adoption and restore my birth mother as my legal parent.

"Let me ask you, if you knew the things that have been brought to light about the adoptive parents and their histories, and about the birth mother's conflicting desires, would your department still have recommended that this adoption go through?"

I think the question surprised Jo, but after a moment she answered thoughtfully, "No, your honor, we would not be able to recommend this adoption with the facts as they sit before us today."

"That's all I need to hear," the judge said.

He turned to me. I was still fuming slightly at being shut down as a participant in my own case, so I spoke out before he could even begin.

"I'd like to know why all of these facts weren't known to the department back at the time of my adoption. The caseworkers could have requested the documents, same as I did." I said

The judge frowned at me.

"I'm not here to answer for why the state did or did not do any particular thing at the time of your adoption. This court has suffered enough damage from this case."

Mallory leaned over to me and whispered, "Mike, stop talking. Don't you get it? We just won."

The judge continued, "Mr. Chalek, I am prepared to properly consider granting your petition. Tell me, what exactly is it that you want?"

Despite the rather abrupt turn of events, I took a deep breath and answered steadily, "I want those people out of my life. Permanently. I want them erased from my birth certificate, and the adoption completely overturned. And I would like the new certificate to show my mother's correct and true name."

The judge asked if Mallory could hand me a piece of blank paper. Mallory quickly obliged.

"Mr. Chalek," Judge Giunta said. "Please write on this page the details of your new birth certificate, exactly as you would like them to appear."

I grabbed the paper and began writing; eventually I had to turn the paper sideways to fit everything in.

Behind me, I could hear Ron Word also scribbling out furious notes.

When I handed the paper back to the judge, he raised his eyebrows in surprise.

"Am I to understand that after all of this, you would like to retain your last name, the name Chalek?" he asked incredulously.

"Your honor, as much as I despise the parents that raised me, and any mention of their names, I cannot sacrifice on the altar of their misdeeds the name I have made for myself as an industry-recognized professional. I have made, and sometimes lost, several fortunes, been interviewed on national news for my professional achievements, and registered copyrights in my name to the software I have designed. I'll bear the last name of Chalek, but I request that any other tie between myself and them be severed forever."

It was a good speech, and the judge accepted my explanation.

He indicated that he would take a couple of weeks to consider the matter and issue his final decision.

After the judge dismissed us all from his chambers, I shook hands with Josette and thanked her profusely for her help. Ron Word stopped me to make sure he had the most recent contact information if he needed to ask any clarifying questions, and I told him I looked forward to seeing his article in the paper the next day.

Mallory explained to me that the judge's final instructions that we would hear his official ruling within a few weeks were just a formality.

"I know Maurice well," he said. "He's going to grant your petition."

Then Mallory and I exited the courthouse, together. Once outside, my old friend began laughing as if we'd just been told the most wonderful joke.

He said. "Mike, you dealt that court one hell of a sucker punch."

"I did not," I said, offended at the implication.

He looked at me piercingly and replied, "Yes, yes you did. And let me tell you why."

I waited, still annoyed but curious nonetheless.

"When you first went into that court and talked to Judge Cates, he asked you why you wanted to unseal your records, what your motivations were. Do you remember what you told him?"

"That I just wanted to find my birth mother," I said.

"That's right. He let you have those records because you were supposed to go find your mom and then disappear and leave the system alone."

"Oh," I said.

"I have a feeling that Judge Giunta is going to track down Robert Cates and give him a swift kick in the behind," Mallory said as he wound himself up to another good chortle.

He slapped me on the shoulder and said, "Let's head home and celebrate."

We got into the rental car, and lit up the cigars that Mallory had brought in case things turned out in our favor.

"You knew this would happen," I accused him as we drove back home.

He just smiled and smoked as we settled in for the long drive ahead.

* * * * * *

On January 02, 2000 I received an email from Mallory with the subject line:

> ***My dear friend! I am happy to start your new century by advising that your long and lonely quest for IDENTITY AND JUSTICE IS OVER.***

He followed it up by saying,

> *In every respect, we won a marvelous victory. You were granted everything you sought. At 9:30 on 1/3/2000 you will receive via fax a copy, with the ORIGINAL order following by mail.*

Here is the text of the entire judgement.

> IN RE: THE ADOPTION OF MICHAEL EDWARD CHALEK
> CASE NO: 6815-C
>
> ORDER GRANTING PETITION FOR

ANNULMENT OF ADOPTION AND AMENDMENT OF CERTIFICATE OF LIVE BIRTH

THIS CAUSE came before the Court on December 13, 1999, upon the "Petition for Annulment of Adoption and Termination of Parental Rights and for Amendment of Certificate of Live Birth" filed by Michael Edward Chalek, adoptee, on June 7, 1999. The petitioner and his counself were present. Josette P Marquess also appeared in her capacity as representative of the Florida Department of Children and Families Adoption Registry. The Court, having reviewed the petition and evidence presented, and having heard testimony of the petitioner and Josette P Marquess, and argument of counsel, finds that an annulment of the adoption of Michael Edward Chalek and the amendment of his certificate of live birth is necessary. However, since both adoptive parents are deceased, the issue of termination of parental rights is moot.

The Court does not make this finding carelessly. The public policy of this State is to protect and respect the privacy of those who so generously decide, for whatever reason, to give to a child the gift of the opportunity to achieve what life has to offer with adoptive parents, and give to the adoptive parents the gift of providing those opportunities to the child. Unfortunately, in the instant case, the adoptive parents abused this privilege and instead caused profound harm to the adoptee. Moreover, but for the adoptive parents' misrepresentation and fraud upon the Court, the Department of Children and Families and/or Judge John A. H. Murphree, who presided over the adoption, would have denied their petition for adoption.

Therefore, the petition for annulment is granted and the Court must provide petitioner with a lawful identity. Petitioner, born during a legitimate marriage, is a child of the marriage under Florida law. At his birth, his biological mother, under duress imposed upon her by the adoption broker, recorded the birth using a fictitious name. Petitioner requests that the certificate be amended to reflect the legal name of the petitioner's biological mother and lawful father at the time of his birth. The Court grants this request and directs that the petitioner's Certificate of Live Birth be amended to reflect the true identity of the biological mother, Winnie Faye Higginbotham Yarber and the lawful father, Thomas Yarber, and further amended to record the child's name as Michael Edward Higginbotham Yarber. However, petitioner asks that his name, Michael Edward Chalek, remain as such since he is known professionally by that name. The Court grants the request and his name shall appear on the Certificate of Live Birth as Michael Edward Chalek. This Court reserves jurisdiction over the subject matter of this case.

ORDERED on this 22nd day of December, 1999.

Epilogue

No human stories ever really end. They just keep switching chapters, and at some point we close one volume and decide to start another.

In this volume of my life there were a few more loose ends that I needed to tie up, or that the universe thought I should tie up, before I was free to move on. One of those was the matter of Carol Jean.

I did what I had sworn to do, and sought out every possible lead in trying to determine what had happened to my little sister. I found distant cousins of hers, called people who had lived in her California neighborhood, and even tracked down her father where he resides in Sweden. He angrily denied having any knowledge of what became of his daughter. I called up Josette Marquess and asked if she had reason to believe that an adoption petition had ever been filed in Florida for Carol Jean Wagner. No such petition existed.

With great sadness, I decided there was nothing more I could do within my limited resources and considering the vast amount of time that had passed since her disappearance.

I also attempted to obtain genetic proof of my

relationship to John Kirchaine, my alleged birth father. John had passed away in the 70s, but he had a brother who was still living. I also talked to a cousin on my father's side who, in another outrageous turn of fate, turned out to be my double cousin. Her father had been another of John's brothers, and her mother was one of Winnie Faye's sisters. When she realized this and explained it to me, I simply shook my head and whispered "very funny," just in case God was listening.

This cousin graciously met me in the Denver airport one day when she was passing through, just so she could give me a few pictures of my father. I never had any DNA evidence to prove or disprove the relationship, but the resemblance between John's pictures and my own are indicative that my mother's claims were probably true.

Speaking of Winnie Faye, she passed away a few years after the court ruling, having been ravaged by the effects of age and end-stage multiple sclerosis. With her passing, I lost all contact with my biological family. I was not even informed of her death until a family friend took pity and called to let me know. He also informed me that my brother Robert and his wife had taken the inheritance and built a large new house elsewhere.

At one point I tried contacting my older brother, Kenneth just to tell him who I was and see if he wanted to meet.

He told me, "I've washed my hands of Winnie Faye, and I have no interest in ever meeting you."

I received a better reception within the vast

adoption community than I received at any time from either of my two families. As a matter of fact, I received a phone call of congratulations from the big man himself—Steve Jobs. He's perhaps the most powerful and famous individual who has ever been involved in a birth mother search, and after we chatted for a moment he asked, in all seriousness, if I might have any advice for him in his own efforts. All I could say was, "Keep trying."

Eventually, though, I was able to help at least one other adoptee gain closure on the question of his origins. At the end of my journey, the story of Rebecca Cobb came full circle. The infant son that Ms. Cobb surrendered for adoption at the time of her lawsuit against Lenora Fielding was now a grown man, searching for his mother. Somehow he had acquired her name but nothing more. He pestered Josette's office in Tallahassee until she took pity and told him that she couldn't personally give him any information, but he might be interested in looking up another adoptee from Jacksonville, a rather famous one whose recent lawsuit had made national headlines.

So the son of Rebecca Cobb and I met up one day, in an airport. I knew from my old investigations into the Fielding operation that Rebecca Cobb had passed away. I had copies of the newspaper articles, the lawsuit and the information from her obituary, which I gave to him. We shook hands, he thanked me, and he disappeared back onto his connecting flight. I can only hope he found some peace along the way.

So here I am, at the end of it all, still an unmoored ship in the sea of humanity. My parents are dead, my siblings have lost interest in any ongoing relationship, and my children are now grown and living their own lives. Many might wonder and ask, "What was the point?"

The point, I would say, is that I now possess the peace of mind that comes with knowing what every non-adopted person takes for granted. I know my identity, my biological history, and the story of my birth. It is my story. No one ever had the right to take it away from me, just because in that moment of relinquishment I was small and helpless and of considerable monetary value on the open market.

I find satisfaction these day in my work, and in trying to bring hope and encouragement to the ongoing fight for open adoption records in all fifty states. Until enough stories have been told, and enough voices have been heard, it is a quest that will not reach its completion.

My time is also filled with whatever good works I see at hand in the moment. I am an active member of Rotary International, a humanitarian organization whose motto is "Service above Self." It is partly through the Rotary that I located my old teacher, Elle Berger, who was responsible for making such a positive difference in the course of my life.

Along with the many volunteer opportunities that Rotary provides me on a regular basis, I felt compelled to make an even larger effort to bring relief to the children of Haiti who were left destitute by the earthquake in 2010. I joined a team and volunteered to take thousands of pounds of supplies that we gathered through joint work with HELP International, another group with whom I frequently partner. Delivering those goods, and seeing the children and their families respond to the hope that the supplies represented, I knew that I would never be whole without the meaning that such acts of service bring into my life.

What does volunteerism do for me?

It's an exercise in compassion.

It's a way to create some good karma.

It keeps me busy.

Most importantly... It keeps me connected.

Mike Chalek in Haiti
with HELP International
2010

CPSIA information can be obtained at www.ICGtesting.com
Printed in the USA
LVOW08s2014101114

412966LV00002B/4/P